STRIPPED D

I0067238

PROJECT
MANAGEMENT

THEORY, PRACTICE,
AND TOOLS FOR

SUCCESSFUL
PROJECT
MANAGERS

JOHN PAYNE

John Payne

Stripped Down Project Management

Theory, Practice, and Tools for Successful Project Managers

Stripped Down Books

www.Stripped-Down-Books.com

Cover Design: Eleonora Kiss

ISBN: 978-3-946160-50-2

Produced by:

Rapid Results GmbH

Käuzchenweg 9

61239 Ober-Mörlen

Germany

Copyright © Rapid Results GmbH

All rights reserved

No part of this book may be reproduced in any form or by any means without prior written permission from the publisher

Contents

Acknowledgements   **xi**

Introduction   **xiii**

Part I   Overview   1

Chapter 1.   What Is Project Management? 2

Chapter 2.   Project Process: An Overview 7

             Initiation...8

             Planning..9

             Execution & Monitoring 10

             Closure 11

             Example 12

Chapter 3.   The Players..15

             The Project Sponsor...16

             The Project Manager...18

             The Project Team 19

             The Project Management Office..20

Part II   The Project Organization   21

Chapter 4.   Introducing the Matrix Organization 22

Resource Conflicts: Line vs. Project...............................29

Chapter 5.   The PMO (Project Management Office)..........................31

Define the Organization's Project Management

Methodology 33

Project Management Training 36

Maintain a Consolidated Status Overview of all

Projects 38

Risk Management...42

Set Standards within the Organization for Projects..44

Agree to the Relative Priorities of Different Projects46

Knowledge Management..49

Where to Place the PMO 51

Chapter 6.   The Project Sponsor..52

Role and Responsibilities...53

Part III   Project Management Theory   61

Chapter 7.   Introduction to Project Management Theory...............62

Chapter 8.   Project Management Process Overview 63

Chapter 9.   Initiation...66

Clarify and Document the Project Goals.......................67

Select and Assign the Project Manager 69

Evaluate the Project Goals 71

Identify the Project Stakeholders 72

Create an Outline Business Case 74

Decision: Commit to Plan the Project 76

Perform the Administrative Actions Required to

Initiate the Project 77

Chapter 10.   Planning 78

Define the Deliverables.. 80

Identify the Resources Required to Deliver the

Project Deliverables 84

Create the Project Plan 87

Create the Detailed Business Case...................... 94

Create the Scope Statement................................... 96

Formally Commit to the Project 98

Chapter 11.   Execution & Monitoring.............................. 99

Formally Starting the Execution and Monitoring

Phase: The Kick-off Meeting............................. 101

Execution 102

Completing Execution 112

Chapter 12.   Closing 113

Formal Handover of the Project Results to the Project

Sponsor.. 114

Lessons Learned 115

Formal Closure 116

Part IV   Project Management Practice   117

Chapter 13.   Introduction to Project Management Practice 118

Chapter 14.   Initiation 120

Clarify the Goals of the Project........................... 123

Select the Project Manager.................................. 126

Define Quality Measures 128

Create an Outline Business Case......................... 131

Identify the Project Stakeholders....................... 133

Contents

Decision: Commit the Resources for Project Planning 135

Perform the Administrative Actions Required to

Initiate the Project 137

Chapter 15.   Project Planning 139

Evaluate the Project Goals 142

Define the Deliverables 143

Estimate the Time and Resources Required to

Complete the Project 146

Create the Project Plan 155

Complete the Business Case 168

Create the Scope Statement 170

Formally Commit to the Project 173

Chapter 16.   Project Execution & Monitoring 177

Complete any Administrative Tasks 179

Hold the Project Kick-off Meeting 180

Distribute Work Packages 183

Execute the Work Packages 184

Monitoring 186

Plan Changes 198

Report Progress 208

Implement Change Requests 214

Respond to Issues 215

Requests for Decisions 227

Management of the Project Team 231

Chapter 17.   Project Closure 241

Formal Handover and Acceptance from the Project

Sponsor 242

Lessons Learned 243

Formal Project Closure 247

Administrative Tasks.. 249

Closing Failed or Incomplete Projects 250

Part V   **Tools**   **253**

Chapter 18.   Creativity 254

Brainstorming... 262

Mind Mapping.. 264

Reversal:.. 267

Applying 5W's and one H.............................. 268

Chapter 19.   The Project Management Triangle................ 270

Chapter 20.   Work Breakdown Structure............................ 273

Chapter 21.   Estimating Techniques..................................... 280

Top Down Estimating..................................... 282

Analogous Estimation 283

Delphi Method 284

Parametric Estimating 286

Bottom up Estimating 288

Expert Estimation 290

Three Point Estimation................................... 292

Chapter 22.   Project Schedule.. 294

Task Dependencies.. 296

Network Diagram.. 300

Gantt Chart... 305

Chapter 23.   Risk Management 309

Identifying Risks:... 313

Contents

Quantifying the Risk:...316

Risk Mitigation Strategies...328

Managing Risk During Project Execution: 331

Chapter 24.   People Management 332

Types of Authority and Power...333

Team Building...335

Skill Management..339

Communication 342

Chapter 25.   Cost Management..350

Simplified Earned Value Management (EVM) 352

Burndown Chart..364

Chapter 26.   Time Management...366

Appendix   371

Work Package Template..372

Communication Plan Template...374

Scope Statement Template...375

Steering Board Report Template..377

Index   383

Tables & Figures

A Typical Line Organization 22

A Typical Project Organizational Structure 25

A Typical Matrix Organization.. 26

Sample Consolidated Project Report........................... 40

Simplified Project Process Summary 64

Resource Usage over Time.. 89

Execution Process Cycle Summary........................... 102

Sample Gantt Chart.. 158

Project Change Types Grouped by Impact and Source... 199

Sample Report Template 211

The Most Frequently Occurring Project Issues................. 216

Sample Decision Request Template........................... 230

Creativity Framework... 256

Example of a Mind Map 266

The Project Management Triangle 270

Work Breakdown Structure 273

WBS in AIL Format.. 275

Contents

Network Diagram Example 302

Gantt Chart 307

Gantt Chart with Progress Bars 308

Example of a Project Risk Register 314

Project Risk Diagram 319

Contingency Cost Table 321

Project Team Performance Over Time 335

EVM: Normal Project Achievement 356

EVM: Normal Project Achievement with Actual Costs Added 358

EVM: Poor Project Performance 359

EVM: Project with Insufficient Resources Committed 360

EVM: Project Over-Performing with Respect to Costs 361

EVM: Project Over-Performing with Respect to the Delivery Schedule 362

The graph below shows a project that is being completed faster than expected. 362

Project Burndown Chart 365

Acknowledgements

This book would not have been possible if I had not had the support of a number of people while I was writing it.

First, I would like to thank all the people and organizations who trusted me to deliver their projects for them. It has been a real pleasure to work together with you.

I would also like to thank the project managers that I have coached or trained. It has been a lot of fun and very rewarding. I am know that I learned just as much from you as you did from me.

For his help, advice, and sense of humor, I would like to thank Jonathan Feist, Editor in Chief of Berklee Press.

On a more personal note, I would like to say a special thank you to my partner, Charys, for her love and support while I wrote this book, as well as for all her work proofreading. Your help and advice have been invaluable.

Finally, a special thank you to our kids: Caitlin, Sam and Ethan, for asking "But, what do you actually do...?"

Introduction

Project management is one of the most exciting disciplines to be working in today. Projects are the place where the new products, services, and processes that we use every day are created. Projects give people an opportunity to show their leadership skills, entrepreneurship, and creativity and are often a springboard for making the next career step.

According to the PMI (Project Management Institute, one of the largest project management organizations worldwide), approximately one fifth of global GDP is being spent on projects. This is about 12 trillion USD a year! For organizations to both grow and remain successful, it is imperative that they manage their projects at least as effectively and efficiently as they manage their daily operations.

Unfortunately, various studies have shown that many organizations struggle to deliver projects successfully. Approximately a third of all projects fail to meet the original business goal and less than 40% of projects are delivered on time and within budget. This book intends to help project managers improve those statistics.

The overall goal of *Stripped Down Project Management* is to reduce the project management process to the most essential tasks. This achieves two main results. First, the workload on the project manager and the project team is reduced, giving them more time to work on creating the project results. Second, stripping away the less productive tasks creates a clearer path through the project management process. This makes it easier for everyone involved in the project to understand what is happening and why.

Many of the project managers I have either coached or trained ran into similar difficulties:

- "Oh my god. I have this project. What do I do next?"
- Struggling to put the theoretical knowledge that they had gained during training to practical use
- Not knowing which tasks need to be prioritized to push the project forward successfully
- Not knowing how to approach putting the project back on track after something went wrong

In *Stripped Down Project Management*, I have addressed these and many similar concerns that project managers have raised with me during coaching sessions.

This book is organized into five parts:

Part I: Overview
Part I provides a summary of the project management process. It is easier to follow the more in-depth parts of the book if you have already understood the core process.

The overview also introduces all the major roles involved in project management and provides a short description of what is expected from the people in each role.

Part II: Introducing the Matrix Organization
Part II looks in more detail at how an organization needs to organize itself so that it can run projects effectively.

The matrix organization, the role of the Project Management Office (PMO), and the role of the Project Sponsor are described here more fully.

Part III: Project Management Theory
Part III concentrates on the theory of project management, with a particular focus on the project management process itself. The intention is to provide a theoretical framework into which the actual practice of project management can be placed.

However, if you find theory less than engrossing and you are mainly focused on the practical side of project management, skip ahead to Part 4: Project Management Practice and refer to Part 3 later if you find you need it.

Part IV: Project Management Practice

Part IV concentrates on the hands-on, practical day-to-day job of delivering a project successfully and effectively. The core content is a clear, step-by-step guide to delivering a project on time, within budget, and at the expected level of quality.

Following the *Stripped Down Project Management* method will keep the project on track without anyone wasting their time on a task which does not add value to the project.

In addition to this, there is advice on when and where to use the tools described in the tools section. Finally, there is advice on how to recover if the project starts to go off plan.

Part V: Tools

Finally, as in any trade, a project manager needs to have a set of tools to work with. A selection of tools has been included to support you as you work through your project. These tools are explained in this section, including a short summary of when, where and why you would want to use them.

Finally, one of the things that I have enjoyed the most during my years as a project manager has been the opportunity to share my knowledge as a trainer and a coach. Through this book, I hope to support you in being a successful project manager.

Part I

Overview

Part I provides a very brief overview of project management. It will be especially useful for anyone who is new to project management. I have frequently found that, before discussing project management in detail, it is useful to have an overview of the following:

- What project management is all about
- The project management process, in particular, the major phases which any project will go through
- The main people involved in delivering a project

CHAPTER 1.

WHAT IS PROJECT MANAGEMENT?

Overview

If you search online for definitions of project management, you will end up with a set of quite formal definitions, some of which do not make much sense unless you have already had quite a lot of project management experience. In simple terms, project management is about bringing a group of people together to achieve a common goal within a set time frame and budget.

What is a project?

Most people have a general idea of the difference between project work and an organization's normal operations. However, it makes sense to be clear about what a project is and how it differs from normal operations.

> **Project:**
>
> A project is temporary. In other words, a project has a beginning and an end.
>
> A project creates something new or unique.
>
> Examples would be the creation of a new product, service, or a result.

A project needs resources to be made available to the project manager so that they can achieve the common goal. Resources in this sense include people, time, money, machinery, work areas, and so on. The resources assigned to it are limited. Therefore, the assigned resources need to be used (managed) as efficiently and effectively as possible to achieve the intended project goals. Otherwise, the project manager is likely to run out of resources before the project has completed its goal!

Typically, a project is a group effort. It often involves people from different parts of an organization who would not normally work closely together. Each person in the team will have a skill, knowledge, or expertise, which the project needs. Being able to manage people with diverse skills and areas of expertise is a significant part of the project manager's role.

A project is temporary. However, temporary does not necessarily mean short. Some large projects may take several years to complete. (Government sponsored construction work, such as building a highway, may take many years to complete.)

Since a project is developing something new, mature operational procedures for the tasks at hand may not exist. This makes it difficult to predict how long delivering the desired project results will take. This uncertainty will lead to an increased level of risk to the organization.

Overview

Some examples of projects would be:

- A town which is initiating a cultural festival for the first time
- Developing a product or service which is new to the organization
- Implementing a quality improvement process where one did not exist before

What are operational tasks?

> **Operations:**
>
> Operations are ongoing. They have no planned end date.
>
> The same products or services are delivered again and again.

In normal operational work, because the same tasks are repeated again and again, the organization will have gained knowledge and experience over time. This knowledge and experience will have been used to develop mature procedures that help to complete the work efficiently and effectively.

Some examples of operations would be:

- Producing a car

- Providing someone with a bank account
- The fire brigade responding to an emergency call

Some operations work may benefit from being organized as if it were a project even though it is not, strictly speaking, a project. This may be the case for work that involves people from different parts of the normal line organization working together in an unusual way. It may also be true, if the risk related to the task is large enough that the executive management team wants to be aware of the status of the work on a regular basis.

What is management?

We have looked at the "project" part of project management. Now let us have a brief look at "management" as well:

> **Management:**
> The Business Dictionary defines management (verb) as "the organization and co-ordination of the activities of the business in order to achieve defined objectives."

This definition fits well into project management. The project manager will organize the people, tools, machinery, workspace, etc. which are necessary to enable people to work together to achieve the common goal.

5

Working together to achieve a common goal is what projects are all about.

CHAPTER 2.

PROJECT PROCESS: AN OVERVIEW

This overview is a short and somewhat idealized summary of completing a project using the *Stripped Down Project Management* process.

Before going into any real depth on how to manage a project, it is useful to have an overview of the project process. As a project moves from start to finish, it will go through a number of phases. These phases are:

- Initiation
- Planning
- Execution & Monitoring
- Closure

INITIATION

Any project will start out with a rough idea of what is to be achieved. This is often considered to be the overall goal of the project.

During initiation, this rough idea is firmed up so that the expected results and benefits (either to the customer or to the organization itself) can be clearly described to everyone who will be involved in the project. In particular, the people who will be planning and/or executing the project will need a very clear idea of what needs to be achieved before they start work. The expected results and benefits should be defined as a set of requirements to be fulfilled by the project team. The focus during this phase will be on *what* the project team needs to deliver and not on *how* they will achieve it.

At the end of the initiation phase, the project is formally started. This means that the organization agrees to commit the resources necessary to plan the project in detail. The project will then be tracked within the organization until it completes.

PLANNING

The planning phase of a project is typically quite short when compared to the duration of the project. During the planning phase, representatives of the project team will sit down together to work out how the expected results and benefits described during the initiation phase could actually be delivered.

The result of these discussions will be a set of work packages describing the tasks to be performed. Each work package will have at least one task to complete and will name the people and other resources required to deliver it. Any dependencies on other work packages will be noted.

In theory (and hopefully in practice as well!), at the end of the planning phase the organization knows exactly what is required to deliver the project successfully. With this information, the project sponsor can make the decision to commit all the necessary resources and start work on delivering the results.

Planning is a critical phase of the project. If the planning is significantly wrong, then it is likely that the project will fail.

EXECUTION & MONITORING

The execution and monitoring phase is where the largest investment in time and resources is made as the project team produces the desired project results.

During execution, the work packages described in the planning phase are distributed, executed, and completed. Any issues (problems) that are discovered during execution are resolved by the project team.

Progress monitoring provides a regular check that the project is delivering the expected results according to plan. More specifically, the monitoring task will check that:

- The work packages are completing on time
- The project is remaining within the expected budget
- The completed work meets the quality expectations that were set at the beginning of the project.

Eventually all the work is completed and the desired goal of the project will have been achieved.

Overview

CLOSURE

The focus during closure is on handing over the results that the project team created, to the project sponsor or the customer for them to use.

It is also important to ensure that any new knowledge gained during the project is made available for use by the organization as a whole.

Overview

EXAMPLE

The project phases listed above can be found in almost any project. So that it becomes clearer how the project phases fit together in real life, let us use building a house as an example:

Initiation:

A family decides to build a house. The initiation phase would include a rough outline of the house sketched on a piece of paper, the number of rooms, etc. and some ideas on where the house should be built.

Once the family has an idea that is defined clearly enough so that it can be communicated to an architect or a construction company, they can make the decision to hire someone to draw up a more detailed building design and plan the construction for them.

Planning:

Planning would involve taking the rough outline to a construction company, or to an architect, to get detailed plans and a cost estimate. The plans would include information such as which resources were required (excavators, builders, plumbers, electricians, roofers, plasterers, etc.) and when they were required.

At the end of the planning phase, the family will have an overview of the costs involved, how long it will take, and what the house will look like. Based on this information, the family can make a decision to move forward and commission the architect or construction company to build the house for them. Alternatively, the family may choose to look for a different construction company, or not to build at all.

Execution & Monitoring:

During the execution and monitoring phase, the house would get built. The various specialist teams would come to the building site with their tools and materials at the right time and work on their given task until they have completed it. There would also be regular checks to ensure that the work had been completed to the correct quality standards, on time, and within the original budget that the family had set aside.

Obviously, there are dependencies between each of the different work package to be completed. (The roofers cannot start work until the walls have been built, for example.) These work packages need to be coordinated so that progress is as continuous as possible, and everything is ready for each specialist team when they are due to start.

Closing:

The family who commissioned the building would check that the house meets the specifications made at the start of the project. (In practice, the family may choose to commission a third party to confirm that the house has been built to the expected quality standard / building regulations as they probably lack the knowledge to check themselves.)

Any legal necessities would be completed so that it was confirmed that the building company had completed their work, the family had paid all the bills, and that the family owned the house and could move in.

The project is complete.

Overview

CHAPTER 3.

THE PLAYERS...

Often, the project manager is the focus of attention for a project. Despite this, no experienced project manager would ever claim to have delivered a project alone.

The team that is required for a project to be delivered successfully is introduced on the following pages.

Overview

THE PROJECT SPONSOR

The project sponsor is arguably the most important person involved in the project. The project sponsor has ultimate responsibility to ensure that the project delivers the results and benefits of the project to the organization. The project sponsor either has personal authority over all the resources required to complete the project, or is otherwise able to ensure that the organization commits all the necessary resources to the project.

To understand the project sponsor's role, it can be useful to think of the project sponsor as the person who is responsible for delivering the results of the project. However, instead of completing the project personally, the project sponsor has assigned a project manager to complete the project on their behalf.

In the example of the house being built, one might at first think of the family commissioning the house as being the sponsor. More accurately, the family would be the customer. The project sponsor would be the person within the construction company who is able to make a statement to the family that:

- The construction company is able to build the house according to the given requirements

- The company has all the necessary resources available to complete the house to the family's satisfaction.

The project sponsor is able to make the "yes" decision to commit the construction company to building the house that the family would like to own.

Overview

THE PROJECT MANAGER

The project manager is responsible for the day-to-day management of the project. The project manager uses the authority and resources provided by the project sponsor to ensure that the desired results of the project are delivered correctly.

The project manager reports the progress of the project to the project sponsor and to any other party with a justified interest in the project. Within the authority provided, the project manager will resolve any project related issues themselves.

In the example above of the family building a house, the family will probably have involved a construction company to coordinate the building work for them. The construction company will typically provide a site manager who will take on the day-to-day tasks of ensuring that the building is completed properly.

Overview

THE PROJECT TEAM

The rest of the project team will be made up of people who have the expert knowledge or specialized skills that are necessary to complete the project. It is the project team, under the guidance of the project manager, who will actually deliver the desired results that the project was created to produce.

During the time that the experts are committed to completing project tasks, they report to the project manager. The project manager will assign tasks to the various team members so that, together, they will create the desired project results.

Overview

THE PROJECT MANAGEMENT OFFICE

The PMO (Project Management Office) supports the organization and the project managers by helping them to manage all the projects within the organization.

The PMO is there to help ensure project management quality standards are met, knowledge gained during projects is made available to the organization as a whole and to improve the organization's ability to deliver projects.

The PMO may also be asked by the executive management team to maintain an overall view of the risk to the organization from all the currently active projects.

Overview

Part II

The Project Organization

Organizational structure is something that most of us take for granted and do not question. However, by introducing projects into an organization, the organizational structure is temporarily changed. It is important to be aware of this change and understand how it affects both the organization and the projects being delivered.

CHAPTER 4.

INTRODUCING THE MATRIX ORGANIZATION

Most people work in organizations that are structured in lines. Consider the diagram below. The diagram shows a fairly typical organizational chart for an organization with a line structure.

A Typical Line Organization

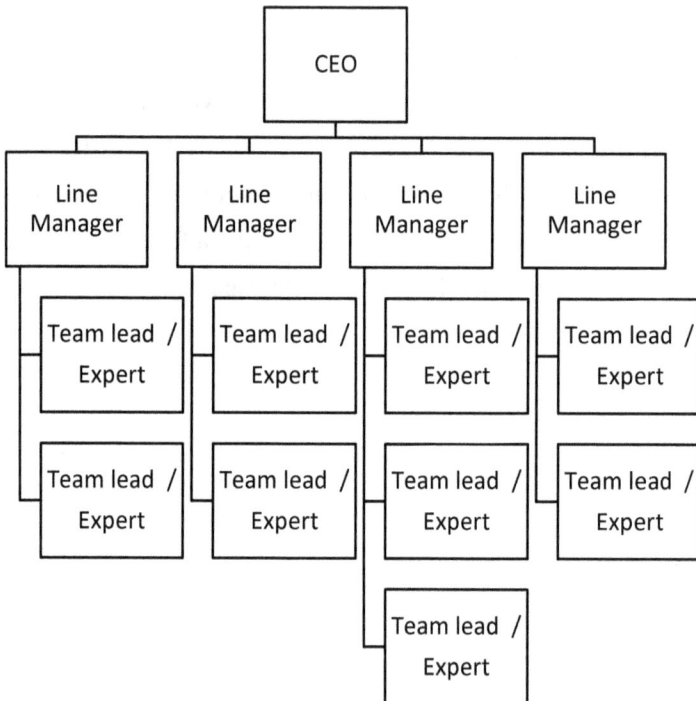

As the previous diagram shows, in a typical line organization there is a CEO (Chief Executive Officer). Reporting directly to the CEO are the line managers. The line managers have functional experts or team leaders reporting to them. The experts create the results that the line is responsible for delivering.

In a line organization, people with similar specializations normally work together. This enables them to share experiences and the organization as a whole improves because of it. Particularly in a medium to large organization, people working in one line of the organization may have little or no contact with people working in a different line. They may even be only vaguely aware of what they do.

The head of each line typically has detailed knowledge of the capabilities of their line. They understand the work that is being performed, as well as having a good understanding of how the work being produced by the line supports the organization in general.

At the CEO level, there is typically a broader understanding of the whole organization, but some of the detailed knowledge required for day-to-day activities is not present.

The Project Organization

This organizational structure has proven itself to be excellent at delivering good operational performance, time and time again.

Projects, however, are not operations. To achieve the desired project results, people from different functional areas are brought together under the leadership of a project manager. This change of leadership means that the previously existing organizational structure is replaced with a new one.

The project structure includes:

- The project sponsor, who is the "CEO" of the project
- The PMO, which provides a support function to the project team
- The Project Manager, who is the project's "line manager" and is responsible for ensuring that the team works together to produce the project results
- The project team, who are the functional experts and specialists that will work together to deliver the project results

Refer to the diagram below for an example.

The Project Organization

A Typical Project Organizational Structure

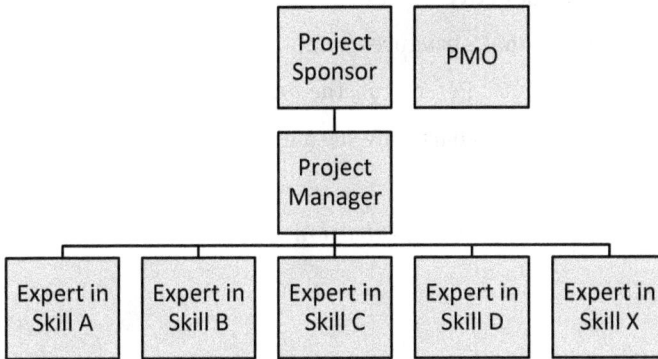

```
        ┌──────────┐  ┌──────────┐
        │ Project  │  │   PMO    │
        │ Sponsor  │  │          │
        └──────────┘  └──────────┘
        ┌──────────┐
        │ Project  │
        │ Manager  │
        └──────────┘
 ┌────────┬────────┬────────┬────────┬────────┐
┌────────┐┌────────┐┌────────┐┌────────┐┌────────┐
│Expert in││Expert in││Expert in││Expert in││Expert in│
│ Skill A ││ Skill B ││ Skill C ││ Skill D ││ Skill X │
└────────┘└────────┘└────────┘└────────┘└────────┘
```

In a project organization, experts from different parts of
the organization are brought together into one team. The
experts in the team are likely to come from completely
different skill or knowledge areas. For example, it would
not be unusual to have a project team that includes people
from Marketing, Sales, Design, Engineering, and
Production.

The team members are brought together to improve
communication and coordination of project tasks as well
as to ensure a clear responsibility for delivering the
project results.

The two organizational forms, the normal operations line
organization and the project organization, are clearly at
odds with each other. In the line organization, the expert

The Project Organization

25

reports to their line manager. In the project organization, the expert reports to the project manager. Normally, the most productive solution is to combine the two organizational structures temporarily to create a matrix organization. Refer to the diagram below for an organizational chart showing a matrix organization.

A Typical Matrix Organization

The Project Organization

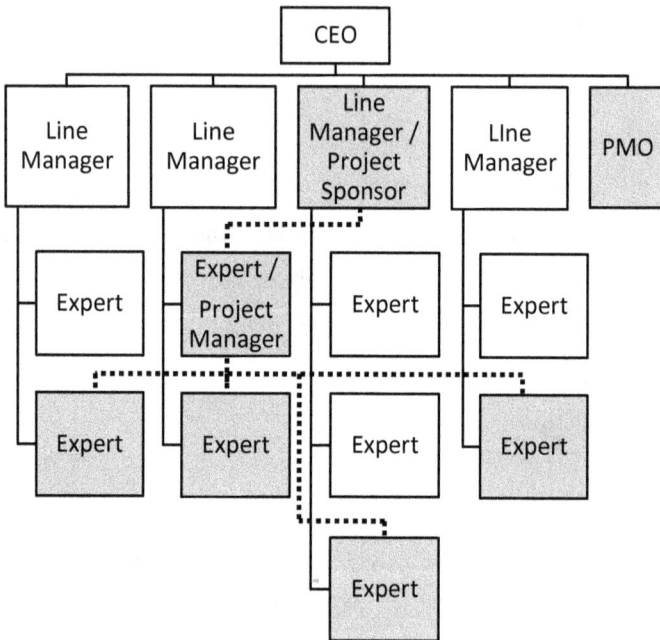

The grey boxes represent the staff involved in the project organization. The dotted lines represent the reporting structure inside the project organization.

In a matrix organization, for the duration of the project, the experts involved in the project will have two lines of reporting:

- To their normal line manager: for any still existing daily operational tasks
- To the project manager: for all project related tasks

The Advantages and Disadvantages of Matrix Organizations

As with any organizational structure, the matrix organization has both advantages and disadvantages.

One practical advantage of a matrix organization is that it allows a project to be managed without disrupting the existing line organization. A person who is assigned to a project does not need to be reassigned by the HR (Human Resources) department to a new manager and then be reassigned back again once the project has completed. Indeed, the specialist may not even be committed 100% to the project. Instead, they may only be assigned to the project for some percentage of their time each week and, during their remaining available time, they would continue to be expected to complete other tasks assigned to them by their line manager.

The Project Organization

This has obvious advantages to both the line organization and the expert aside from solving the problems that would be associated with frequently reassigning experts to different managers. The line manager is still able to call upon the expert's knowledge and skill should they need to do so. For the expert, it means that they do not lose track of new developments within their own line organization.

The main disadvantage of the matrix structure is the possibility for conflict between two reporting lines. The line manager may request that a specialist perform one task, and the project manager may request that the same expert perform a different task at the same time. These two requests are likely to be in conflict with each other and the specialist will need to manage the two different requests in some way.

Matrix organizations are considered to be unstable organizational structures. From a project management point of view, this is desirable. The project organization only needs to exist for the duration of the project. Once the project has completed, the project organization is no longer required and will need to be disbanded.

Some organizations always have a number of projects running at any one time. For these organizations, the organizational structure is continuously in a state of flux, changing to meet the needs of the different projects as they start and end.

RESOURCE CONFLICTS: LINE VS. PROJECT

As briefly discussed in the section above, *The Advantages and Disadvantages of Matrix* Organizations, having two reporting lines for employees creates the possibility of conflicts of interest. Here are two common examples:

- An issue in day-to-day operations can cause a line manager to demand that staff committed to a project support the line operation instead
- An issue in the project may require that a particular expert is required to commit additional, unplanned hours to the project, or to commit hours at a time that deviates from the original schedule

From the point of view of the skill expert, they now have two command and communication lines. The expert will need to manage the demands and workload from both their project manager and their line manager. In most organizations, there will be a tendency for the skill expert to place extra importance on the line manager's demands, because the line manager has disciplinary power over the skill expert while the project manager typically does not.

Few organizations today have so many skilled people and other resources available that no conflicts of interest occur. To resolve conflicts of interest, it is important that there is a clear understanding within the organization of

The Project Organization

the relative importance resolving operational issues and delivering project results. This clarity should come from the executive management team of the organization to ensure that it is supported by all the line managers involved.

The Project Organization

CHAPTER 5.

THE PMO (PROJECT MANAGEMENT OFFICE)

The role of the PMO (Project Management Office) is to support projects throughout the organization. That is easily said, but it is a very vague definition. What does it actually mean in practice?

The main tasks of the PMO are to:

- Define the organization's project management methodology
- Ensure that project managers receive the training and support that they require in order to be successful
- Maintain an overview of all projects, their status, and resourcing requirements
- Create an overview of the risk profile which the ongoing projects are exposing the organization to
- Set standards for project management
- Agree to the relative project priorities with the executive management team and to use this information to assist in resolving resource conflicts

The Project Organization

- Ensure that knowledge and skills developed during project execution are made available to other projects and to the rest of the organization

On the following pages, we will examine each of these tasks in more detail.

DEFINE THE ORGANIZATION'S PROJECT MANAGEMENT METHODOLOGY

The organization's project management methodology will be developed and refined by the PMO. When developing a project management methodology, most organizations go through three major phases of project management maturity: informal, formal, and experienced:

Phase 1: Informal

The first phase of project management maturity is very informal with no clear project management controls.

There is typically no planned status reporting other than the requestor poking their head around the office door and asking if everything is going well. There is no formal resource allocation. Project managers are expected to use their own personal gravitas and influence to be able to deliver the project successfully.

This can be quite successful for very small projects. However, this type of project management methodology typically fails if any serious obstacle presents itself.

Phase 2: Formal

As the project size and complexity increases, the organization recognizes a need for a more formal approach to project management. One of the well-known

The Project Organization

project management methodologies is adopted and some people within the organization receive formal training in project management. This typically improves the quality of the project management dramatically and leads to a corresponding increase in the organization's ability to deliver larger and more complex projects on time and within budget.

Phase 3: Experienced

The final maturity phase is when the organization begins to tailor the project management methodology to fit its own requirements.

As the organization gains more and more experience in delivering projects, it comes to realize that while the selected methodology provides definite benefits to the organization, it is not always a best fit. The organization then starts to develop its own project management best practices. These focus on picking out the parts of the methodology that are relevant and supportive to their organization, industry, and wider environment. Next, additional tools that the organization requires but which the originally chosen methodology did not provide are found elsewhere or developed internally.

In this final maturity phase, the organization has developed its own project management methodology. It is based loosely on the methodology originally implemented and is continually improving according to the organization's own needs and experience.

PROJECT MANAGEMENT TRAINING

The PMO is responsible for ensuring that the organization is not put at unnecessary risk due to poor project management.

To meet this responsibility effectively the PMO needs to ensure that project management training is provided for any new project manager in the organization. This is best controlled centrally in order to maintain consistency within the organization. This can be done in many different ways, including::

- Ensure that all Project Managers attend the same training course
- Provide internal training courses
- Ensure that all Project Managers have read, and use, the same book on project management. (Preferably this book, of course...)

Providing support in the form of mentoring or coaching for new project managers will help them to get up to speed quickly on how projects are run within the organization. Coaching is also particularly helpful for project managers as they make the jump from understanding project management in theory to implementing projects in practice, or when dealing with a problem project.

As part of the process of ensuring that projects are delivered at the level of quality required by the organization, the PMO will need to audit a certain number of projects each year. In addition to ensuring a high level of quality, these audits also:

- Enable the PMO to improve the implemented project management methodology
- Help project managers to improve their skills

The Project Organization

MAINTAIN A CONSOLIDATED STATUS OVERVIEW OF ALL PROJECTS

Most organizations have several projects active at any one time. Each of these projects will have a different goal. Many will have different project sponsors.

The executive management team of an organization should have an overview of all the significant projects that are currently active within the organization. Such an overview assists the executive management team in two ways: First, it provides them with a clear view of the risks to which the organization is exposed. Second, it provides information regarding the overall resources currently committed to active projects. This second point is valuable because the executive management team will need confirmation that sufficient resources remain available to maintain daily operations before considering starting any additional projects.

As discussed further in *Agree to the Relative Priorities of Different Projects* on page 46, separate projects may require access to the same resources. An overview of all the ongoing projects, which includes their relative priority within the organization, makes it possible to resolve conflicts of interest between projects easily.

Maintaining an overview of the current projects would seem to be a relatively simple task. However, particularly in larger organizations or organizations running a lot of smaller projects, getting a central overview of all the ongoing projects can be a serious challenge.

The PMO should be informed every time a project starts and ends. The PMO should also receive a copy of the project steering board report every time it is produced. If the steering board report has a common format, then it is a much easier task to maintain a consolidated project status report, which includes a short summary text with the current status for each project. Additional space in the report can be used to detail the issues associated with projects that are in delay.

The executive management team can review the consolidated project status report regularly. This will keep them aware of problem projects and the remediation actions being taken to correct those problems, as well as making it easier to assign or review the relative priorities assigned to each project.

The Project Organization

Sample Consolidated Project Report

Consolidated Project Report

Project overview

- Top projects:
  - 1 red project. Remediation plan in place. No further support requested.
  - 2 green projects.
  - No open support requests

- Projects
  - 1 red project. Remediation plan in place. No further support requested.
  - 1 amber project. Support request delivered
  - 2 green projects.
  - 1 open support request

Top Projects

Project	PM	Description	Status
ICT Cost opt.	M. White	Reduce the costs for ICT by 15% to year end	● ●
Phonograph	T. Edison	New product: Sound recording innovation	● ● ●
Light Alloy	B. Wallis	Light alloy development for aircraft construction	● ●

Projects

Project	PM	Description	Status
QPO	A. Smith	Improve production quality in Product One.	● ●
Market X	J. Blogs	Develop, test, and implement marketing strategy X	● ●
Opt. Prod 7	W. Green	Optimise production process for product 7	● ●
IT-Net	P. Branath	Redesign IT Network structure	● ●

When reviewing a number of projects, the use of a simple color code (red, yellow, or green) helps to give a very quick overview of the status of the currently active projects.

Some management teams prefer to have a section in the report that gives a short status overview of every project. Almost all management teams are interested to know about the remediation actions being taken to support projects that are not progressing according to plan.

The Project Organization

RISK MANAGEMENT

If the organization's executive management has chosen to manage risk centrally, then it is normally the PMO's role to provide them with the details of the risk profile for the currently active projects.

Typically, the organization's executive management team will be interested to know:

- What is the overall risk to the organization and is this in line with what the executive management team considers to be acceptable?
- Are there any specific risks that the executive management team should be aware of, or possibly even be involved in the management of?
- Are there any particular opportunities that the organization could or should be taking advantage of?

Assuming the PMO is responsible for reporting the current risk profile to the executive management team, the PMO will need to set guidelines and standards for the project managers regarding which risks need to be reported back to the PMO. Guidelines could include:

- Financial risk above a particular sum
- The possibility of damage to the organization's reputation

- The possibility of non-delivery or late delivery of any significant service or order to a (major) customer

The PMO needs to collect the relevant data and present it in a form that is readily understood by the executive management team. The executive management team will normally be interested in the following risk related information:

- Understanding how the organization's risk profile is changing
- What the current major risks are and understanding the steps being taken to manage those risks
- Being informed when previously discussed risks have been avoided or resolved and are no longer a concern

The Project Organization

The Project Organization (sidebar)

SET STANDARDS WITHIN THE ORGANIZATION FOR PROJECTS

The PMO has the role of setting project management standards within the organization.

Every organization will need to strike a balance between implementing standards that help the organization to deliver project successfully, and standards that stifle creativity and innovation.

Some standards that are likely to have a positive impact on the ability of the organization to manage a number of projects simultaneously are:

- Standard project document templates
  Implementing a set of standard templates for the most common project documents makes it easier for the various project stakeholders to find the information that they are looking for. They reduce the workload on the project managers (or other document authors) creating the required project documentation and they help to improve the quality of the available project documentation in general.
- Documentation repository
  Having the results of a similar, previous project available is a valuable source of information when estimating the resources required for a new project. Project managers searching old project

archives for information pertinent to a current project will find it easier if a central document repository is available.

Additionally, a common repository with a standard structure helps to protect the organization against the risk that the project manager may suddenly become unavailable. In this case, another project manager can quickly find the current project status and take over with minimum disruption to the project.

- Guidelines on risk management

Creating a set of guidelines for all projects with regard to acceptable levels of risk and advice on best practice for dealing with particular types of risk, helps the organization to manage overall risk.

AGREE TO THE RELATIVE PRIORITIES OF DIFFERENT PROJECTS

Similar to the conflicts of interest discussed in *Resource Conflicts: Line vs. Project* on page 29, it is possible that two projects will both require access to some of the same resources. Often, the same top experts in the organization are requested to support several different projects at the same time.

This can cause conflicts between projects when work is unable to progress on project A due to the required resources being committed to project B. In some extreme cases, a single person or resource may be committed to so many different projects that no significant progress can be made on any of them.

This situation needs to be recognized and the resources assigned to the higher priority project. To assist in this, it has proven to be very helpful for the executive management team to publish their view of the relative priorities between projects. The organization's executive management team has a holistic view of the entire organization. They are in the best position to be able to decide upon the relative strategic priorities within the organization. In the event that the relative strategic priorities within the organization need to change, then the executive management team is best placed to recognize this and respond accordingly.

Having the executive management team publish its view on the relative project priority within the organization frequently speeds up the resolution of resource conflicts between projects. In many cases, the resource conflicts can be avoided completely.

If an organization has a large number of projects active at any one time, it may not be sensible to try and assign the relative priorities of every project. It may be far more productive to split the projects into three categories:

"Top" projects: The strategically or financially most important projects with the highest priority for the organization

"Normal" projects: Important projects that need to be delivered on time, but not as strategically or financially important as the top projects are

"Nice to have" projects: Projects that are to be completed if the necessary resources are available

Obviously, if one particular project is being delayed because a higher priority project has made the required resources unavailable, then this needs to be highlighted in the project steering board report. If the lower level project becomes unacceptably delayed then the executive management team and the project sponsor will need to be informed. As the project status slips from green to yellow to red, the executive management team may decide to reassign project priorities, organize additional resources, reschedule the project, or even just cancel the project entirely as appropriate.

The PMO should protect the executive management team as much as possible by communicating the management viewpoint to the relevant project managers and project sponsors. In the event of a conflict, the PMO should facilitate a solution via the project sponsors if possible. However, if insufficient information is available to resolve the conflict and an agreement cannot be reached, then the PMO has the job of pointing out the conflict to the executive management team and presenting the impact of the available options. The executive management team then has the job of deciding how the conflict should be resolved.

KNOWLEDGE MANAGEMENT

The first time a new product, process, or service is created, the organization gains fundamental knowledge. For an organization to get the most benefit of this knowledge, it is important that the knowledge learned is captured and distributed to all those who would benefit from it.

Since projects are typically the vehicle used to create a new product, process, or service, then knowledge management is an important part of running a project.

It is part of the PMO's role to ensure that the project manager captures knowledge as part of the project results. The PMO and the project sponsor will support the project manager in making the knowledge available to those who will benefit from it.

Knowledge and experience about the project process needs to be made available or actively shared with other project managers and other people involved in the delivery of similar projects in the future.

Knowledge and experience gained regarding the project results needs to be passed on to the relevant operational or expert teams.

The PMO is responsible for ensuring that projects are not closed without a final "lessons learned" session with the results being documented and acted on where appropriate.

WHERE TO PLACE THE PMO

Returning to our discussion on organization structure from page 22, it is worth considering where to place the PMO within the organization.

For organizations running a significant number of medium- or large-sized projects of strategic value to the organization, it makes sense to have the PMO report directly to the executive management team.

For organizations with fewer projects, or projects of less strategic value to the organization, then it makes sense to include the PMO within the line of the organization that contains the support functions (HR, Finance, etc.).

In rare cases where one functional area is responsible for almost all the projects which the organization runs and provides most of the resources required to deliver those projects, it can make sense to have the PMO in that functional area. If this is not the case, then placing the PMO under the control of one specific functional area can cause problems. The line manager of the functional area concerned is likely to place a higher priority on the projects that directly affect their own line. This will create a biased view of the importance of that particular line's projects within the organization and it is recommended to avoid this option in general.

The Project Organization

CHAPTER 6.

THE PROJECT SPONSOR

As stated earlier, the project sponsor is one of the most important people involved in a project, if not the most important. It is also one of the least well-defined roles in project management literature. Indeed, most literature on project management barely touches on the topic. This is strange since many experienced project managers (including me), would say that having solid support from a capable and effective project sponsor is a key success factor in delivering a project on time and within budget.

In many organizations, the role of the project sponsor is not clearly defined. Even if the role is clearly defined, the project sponsor may be unable (due to lack of time or experience) to fulfill the role. In these cases, it is particularly important that the project manager understands the role of the project sponsor, because they will need to either steer the project sponsor or perform the tasks themselves.

ROLE AND RESPONSIBILITIES

The project sponsor has ultimate responsibility for the successful delivery of the project.

It may be helpful to think of the project sponsor as being the person who would have delivered the project results themselves, if only they had the time available to do so. Since they do not have the time themselves, they have chosen instead to delegate the task to a project manager who will represent them.

The project sponsor will need to select a project manager with the appropriate skills to act on their behalf. The project sponsor remains responsible throughout the project for ensuring that the project manager is doing their job correctly. If the project sponsor realizes that the project manager is not doing their job properly, then the project sponsor will need to either provide the project manager with additional support or replace them with someone more capable.

The project sponsor will need to support the project manager throughout the entire project. Most obviously, the project sponsor will need to ensure that all the necessary resources are made available to the project manager so that the project tasks can be completed.

The Project Organization

Ideally, the project sponsor has enough authority from their position within the organization so that all the resources required to deliver the project are under their personal control. Frequently, this means that the project sponsor is a senior manager or even a member of the executive management team. If the project is being sponsored by someone without full personal control of all the required resources, then the project sponsor will need to liaise with other managers to ensure that all the required resources will be made available for the full duration of the project.

Perhaps not quite so obviously, the project sponsor can support the project manager by sharing their knowledge and experience. The project sponsor will typically have a deeper knowledge of customer's needs, the industry in general, and the organization specifically than the project manager does. Sharing this knowledge will help the project manager and other members of the project team.

Typical ways in which a project sponsor can further support a project manager include:

- Provide some form of coaching or mentoring for the project manager. This may be delivered as advice during the project steering meeting or during a formal coaching session
- Make introductions to people who can support the project manager in completing the project

- Organize training or guidance on organizational processes which are necessary to the project but which are outside of the project manager's experience

The project sponsor has the task of championing the project within the organization. This will help get the support necessary to ensure that the project has the best possible chance of success.

The project sponsor is the interface between the project team and the organization's management team. This involves creating and maintaining awareness, at senior management level, of the project and the benefits that the project is expected to produce. Increasing awareness may require the presentation of a progress summary report regularly to the executive management team, or it may simply require the project sponsor to speak positively about the project in general discussion. The goal is to ensure that there is continued support for the project throughout the lifetime of the project. Particularly if a project is working through a number of unexpected issues, this continued support is essential to complete the project successfully.

Because the project sponsor is responsible for providing the necessary budget and resources, the project sponsor will need to approve the plans created by the project manager. Similarly, any changes to the project scope or deliverables will need to be approved by the project sponsor.

The tasks of the project sponsor during each phase of the project are summarized below.

Project Sponsor Tasks - Initiation:

As one would expect, the project sponsor is typically more intensely involved during the initiation phase of the project than at any other time in the process. The project sponsor's tasks are:

- To ensure that the projects goals, or requirements (the external view of the project), are clearly understood. "Clearly understood" means that they are defined specifically enough that the experts involved in planning and execution will understand unambiguously what the project team needs to deliver
- Assign a project manager with the necessary skills to complete the project
- Create an outline business case
- Perform the administrative tasks necessary to start the project
- Identify the project's most important stakeholders
- Make the decision to commit the necessary resources to complete the planning phase

Project Sponsor Tasks – Planning:

The main planning effort is performed by the project manager and the project team. However, the project sponsor will need to approve the plans, budget requirements, and resource requirements because the project sponsor will be responsible for providing these resources during the execution phase. The project sponsor's tasks are to:

- Approve the project plan, the work packages, and the related budget. The project plan includes the schedule, resource plan, communication plan, and the risk mitigation plan (if required)
- Ensure that the deliverables (internal view of the project) defined by the project team will meet the project goals / requirements (external view of the project) as defined by the project requestor.
- Approve the detailed business case
- Confirm that the project is aligned with the interests of the organization
- Assist the project manager in sourcing the necessary resources
- Approve or reject the project scope statement
- Make the decision whether or not to commit the resources necessary to execute the project successfully

The Project Organization

Project Sponsor Tasks – Execution and Monitoring:

The execution and monitoring tasks should be performed by the project team and the project manager. In an ideal world, the project sponsor would be able to stay in the background, just confirming with the project manager that the project is progressing according to plan or supporting the project manager by providing a quick decision and/or offering some pertinent advice.

In practice, the project will benefit if the project sponsor is more actively involved during execution. The project sponsor is in a better position to maintain a "big picture" view of the overall goals of the project than the project manager, who may get swamped in day-to-day issues. Therefore, it is highly recommended that the project sponsor maintain regular contact with the project manager to ensure that the project focus remains on the tasks necessary to deliver the expected results. The project sponsor's tasks are:

- To approve / deny change requests.
  If the project sponsor approves a project change request, then they also need to ensure that any necessary additional resources are made available to the project manager and that any related delay in delivery is justified and communicated to the relevant stakeholders.

- To read the project reports and ensure that the project manager is making progress as expected. If this is not the case, the project sponsor needs to support the project manager to get the project back on track.
- To respond quickly to any decision requests presented by the project manager
- To champion the project at senior management level
- To manage the contact with the customer or the project requestor

Project Sponsor Tasks – Closure:

The project sponsor will have an active role in the project closure. Once the project results have been made available, the project sponsor will need to confirm that the project results meet the project requirements and fulfill the overall project goals.

Once confirmed, the project results will need to be handed over to the customer or other recipient of the project results for their use. The project sponsor's tasks are:

- To confirm that all the expected deliverables are now available – including any documentation
- To ensure that any improvements from the project's "Lessons learned" are implemented into the organization

- Gather acceptance from the customer / project requestor that the project results meet the project goals / requirements and that the project has been completed
- Ensure that all costs have been booked against the project cost code (if this was required) and close down the cost code

Part III

Project Management Theory

CHAPTER 7.

INTRODUCTION TO PROJECT MANAGEMENT THEORY

The purpose of this part on project management theory is to provide an overall framework into which the practical day-to-day tasks can be placed. It explains the purpose of each of the steps in the project management process and the relationships between them.

This part on theory presents an "ideal world" view of project management. We all know that theory and practice do not always match, so *Part IV Project Management Practice* deals with the more practical "real world" task of delivering a project successfully. However, understanding the theory is often a big help in both keeping an overview of where you are in the project process and prioritizing your workload in a practical situation.

Finally, Part 3 and Part 4 are written so that they can be read independently. So, if theory is really not your thing, then jump ahead to *Part IV Project Management Practice* to get some practical advice on delivering your project successfully and efficiently now. You can come back to this part later on if you find you need it.

CHAPTER 8.

PROJECT MANAGEMENT PROCESS OVERVIEW

The fundamental idea behind project management theory is that, while each individual project is unique and creates a unique end result, product, or service, the process which is followed to implement each project is the same (or if not exactly the same, then similar).

As presented in *Part I*, *Overview*, the project management process is, at its core, a linear process. First, during initiation, there is the conception of what is to be achieved. This is followed by a planning phase where an investigation is done to identify in more detail which tasks need to be completed and which resources would be required to complete the project over which length of time. Next, the project is executed and progress is monitored. Finally, during closing, the completed project results are given to the project sponsor. The project sponsor in turn hands these results over to whoever needed them. This could be a customer, someone within the organization, or some other group of people the project is intended to benefit.

Project Management Theory

Simplified Project Process Summary

The project management methodology presented in this book has a two-phase project approval process. There is an initial approval given at the end of the initiation phase to commit the resources necessary to plan the project. This is followed by a second approval at the end of the planning phase to commit the resources necessary to execute and complete the project.

Some alternative project management methodologies only require a single project approval to be given at the end of the initiation phase of the project. The advantages of this two-phase approach are:

- The project-planning phase is under the control of the project sponsor. It is clear which investment is being made to plan the project and when the project planning results are expected to be delivered

- By postponing the decision to execute the project until after the planning phase has completed, the project sponsor has detailed planning information available. This improved planning information enables a more informed decision on whether or not the project should be executed.

64

- The additional accuracy of having the completed the planning phase before the commitment is made to execute the project, means that the project is far more likely to be completed on time, in quality and within budget

Note that at a more detailed level, parts of the process are definitely repetitive. For example, the execution and monitoring phase has a cycle of steps that are continually executed until all the tasks have been completed.

Project Management Theory

CHAPTER 9.

INITIATION

The initiation phase of project management is where all the necessary preparations are completed so that the project can officially be moved into the planning phase. At the end of the initiation phase, the project sponsor will have sufficient information available to make the decision to commit the necessary resources to complete the planning phase of the project.

This is the project phase where the project sponsor is most visibly in the lead for the project. The project sponsor will be defining the parameters of the project and winning support within the organization.

The main tasks that need to be performed during initiation are:

- Clarify and document the project goals
- Select and assign a project manager to the project
- Evaluate the project goals
- Identify the project stakeholders
- Create an outline business case
- Decision: commit the resources to plan the project or cancel/postpone the project
- Perform the administrative tasks necessary to formally start the project within the organization

CLARIFY AND DOCUMENT THE PROJECT GOALS

The original idea that leads to the project being initiated may come from a number of sources:

- A customer request
- A legal requirement
- An idea from a member of the team / department
- An interpretation of the organization's strategy
- Someone's idea on how to improve something which the organization does

In many cases, this original idea is typically more of a vague vision than a clearly defined goal, so it is important that the idea is refined and made more explicit. The overall project goal needs to be clearly understood by everyone involved in any phase of the project. Without a common, clear understanding of the goal that the project is meant to achieve, it is unlikely that the project will end up delivering the desired results.

In general, the project goal is refined when the following are true:

- The goal can be clearly communicated
- The project exit criteria are clearly defined.
  This is particularly important for projects in which everyone will have their own interpretation of when the task is complete.

Project Management Theory

Typical examples of this are improving product or service quality, raising customer satisfaction, and improving performance.

- A time frame
  Either the expected duration of the project or the expected completion date are known
- Some indication of the relevant cost parameters are available
- The level of quality expected is described in a way that it can be objectively measured
- In cases where a partial project completion would be acceptable, task prioritization. In other words, which tasks must be completed for the project to complete successfully and which tasks should only be performed if there is sufficient time and budget available to complete them

Project Management Theory

SELECT AND ASSIGN THE PROJECT MANAGER

The project manager will manage the project on a day-to-day basis on behalf of the project sponsor. Therefore, the project manager selected must be someone that the project sponsor can trust to complete the project successfully on their behalf. Completing the project successfully means that the project team is able to deliver all the expected project results to the expected level of quality on time and within budget by using the agreed resources.

There are many factors that could be considered when selecting a project manager:

- Do they have sufficient experience to manage a project of this size?
- Do they have the background knowledge that would be helpful or necessary to deliver the project successfully?
- Are they able to work autonomously?
- Will they be accepted by the project team as being capable of managing the project?
- Are they able to communicate to all the project stakeholders clearly?
- Are they able to motivate the project team to produce the desired results without relying solely on the project sponsor's authority?

Project Management Theory

Since the "perfect candidate" is probably not available, then the project sponsor will need to decide which factors are the most important for the success of this project and select the best possible candidate from those available.

If the project sponsor does not have a suitable candidate available, then the next step is to contact the PMO. The PMO may be aware of a suitable candidate in a different part of the organization who fits the project sponsor's most important criteria. If the PMO is also not aware of a suitable candidate for a project manager, then the organization may be forced to source an external candidate to fill the project manager role.

Project Management Theory

EVALUATE THE PROJECT GOALS

The selected project manager will need to review the supplied project goals as written by the project sponsor to ensure that they have understood them clearly.

Any questions that the project manager has regarding the project's goals need to be answered as early as possible in the project lifecycle. In general, the further that a project progresses, the more costly any necessary actions to correct any misunderstandings in the overall project goal will be.

Project Management Theory

IDENTIFY THE PROJECT STAKEHOLDERS

Stakeholders are defined as anyone who could have a legitimate reason to be interested in the project. Depending on the project, this list can be quite large. The immediately identifiable stakeholders are:

- The project sponsor
- Everyone in the project team
- The people who will receive, or make use of, the project results

For some projects, there may be other interested parties:

- The local community
- Special interest groups related to some part of the project
- The industry in which the organization operates
- The organization's competitors

It is helpful to identify as many project stakeholders as possible. This information will be used during planning to help create the communication plan for the project. When creating a stakeholder list, it can be useful to note if the stakeholder views the project positively or negatively and some indication of the amount of influence the stakeholder has over the project.

Project Management Theory

Generally speaking, it is worth investing some care and effort to keep the support of the people who are supporting the project. It is however, also worth taking the time to consider how best to ensure that non-supporters do not stop the project from achieving its goal. Careful management of people negatively impacting the project can contain their impact and possibly even turn them into supporters.

Project Management Theory

CREATE AN OUTLINE BUSINESS CASE

In general, a project has a business case related to it. The project is worth considering if the benefit to the organization is greater than the cost of completing the project. At this phase of the project, only a basic understanding of the business case parameters will be available because the full costs of the project to the organization will not be known until the planning phase has been completed. Despite this, making the outline business case available to the planning team will help them to produce a plan that is more likely to be acceptable to the project sponsor and in line with the organization's overall goals.

Sometimes a formal business case may not be necessary. For example, if the organization needs to deliver a particular function or service in order to meet new legislative requirements, then the business case becomes, perform the project or stop doing business.

Another example could be that the organization decides to commit a certain amount of their available development budget to a particular new product or feature. For low cost developments, the costs of a market analysis to identify the expected profit may be higher than the cost of the development itself. For very innovative developments, the results of a market analysis may be too unreliable for a meaningful business case to be developed. In each of these cases, no reliable data would be available for a formal business case.

DECISION: COMMIT TO PLAN THE PROJECT

At the end of the initiation phase, the project sponsor needs to decide if the project has merit and should move to the planning phase. In the planning phase, more detailed information will be made available, which will enable a fully informed decision to be made on whether or not to execute the project.

Therefore, the end of the initiation phase of the project is marked by making the first "go / no go" decision for the project. The project sponsor will decide if the necessary resources should be committed to create a planning team and perform a detailed planning of the project.

To support the decision making progress, at the end of the initiation phase of the project the project sponsor should have the following information available:

- The name of a project manager who is available and competent to complete the project
- Clearly defined goals describing what the project is expected to achieve
- A list of the most influential stakeholders in the project and whether they are likely to be supporters or detractors of the project
- An outline business case that describes the general parameters for the project

Project Management Theory

PERFORM THE ADMINISTRATIVE ACTIONS REQUIRED TO INITIATE THE PROJECT

Each organization will have their procedures for formally starting a project. The steps described below make the assumption that there is a central PMO in place as described in the chapter *The PMO (Project Management Office)* on page 31.

Inform the PMO of the Project

The PMO will need to register the project into the organization's central project tracking system. This enables the PMO to maintain their central overview of all projects on behalf of the executive management team including the overall risk to which the organization is exposed. It also enables the PMO to monitor the project and ensure that the project management standard practices for the organization are being followed.

Ensure Cost Tracking is in Place

For any non-trivial project, cost information is valuable for similar projects in the future. So that this information can be collected efficiently and effectively, it is important that cost monitoring is put in place at the start of the project. This avoids the difficulties of attempting to gather the information retrospectively after the project has started (or in some extreme cases – after the project has completed.)

CHAPTER 10.

PLANNING

The overall goal of the planning phase of the project is to provide the project sponsor with sufficient information to enable them to make the decision to commit the necessary resources to complete the project or not.

As a by-product of this planning phase, the project team will create a number of plans that will be used for the execution phase of the project.

The plans created by the project team will identify:

- Which resources need to be committed to the project to achieve the desired results
- Whether or not the required resources are available to the organization
- If appropriate: What would be the impact to the organization on other work if this project were to be started?

The project plans will tell the project sponsor whether or not the project is feasible. Assuming that the project is feasible, the project team will continue to create an initial risk assessment and business case. This will show if completing the project is likely to be beneficial for the organization or not. With this information available, the project sponsor will be able to decide whether or not to commit the necessary resources to complete the project.

The following pages will go through the necessary steps to complete the planning phase of the project. These can be summarized as:

- Define the project deliverables
- Identify the resources required to create the deliverables
    - Split the deliverables into work packages
    - Estimate the time and resources required to complete each of the individual work packages and the project as a whole
    - Confirm that the required resources could be made available to the project
- Create the project plan
    - Delivery Schedule
    - Resource Plan
    - Communication Plan
- Provide an initial risk assessment
- Provide the detailed business case
- Create the scope statement
- Decision: Commit the resources required to execute the project

Project Management Theory

DEFINE THE DELIVERABLES

Often, project goals are defined in the form of business requirements or customer requirements, which the project is expected to fulfill. The requirements are understood by the customer and the project sponsor. They create an external view of what the project will deliver.

The next step is to take this "external view" of the project and turn it into a set of clearly defined deliverables that the project team can create. These deliverables will define the organization's "internal view" of the project. If the project team delivers all of the deliverables defined for the project, then the expectation within the project team and the wider organization will be that the project requirements will have been met.

Example of an internal view and an external view of a project:

A manufacturing company has hired a marketing company to create a marketing campaign. The manufacturing company has set the project goal to be "*Create a marketing campaign to increase sales of product X by at least 15% without reducing the current sales price.*"

The marketing company's project planning team creates a set of in-house deliverables:

- Market research document:

Project Management Theory

Perform market research by contacting people who have bought the product in the past to identify what their view of the main product benefit is. Document the results

- Market analysis document:

  Perform some market analysis based on the market research results, to identify the main target groups of people who are likely to be interested in receiving the benefit provided by the product. Document the results

- Market campaign:

  Create a marketing campaign aimed at the people who are most likely to benefit from the product. The marketing campaign will explain to the target groups what benefit they would gain by purchasing the manufacturing company's product

- Marketing campaign signoff:

  Get agreement from the manufacturing company that the marketing campaign is suitable and will be used

- Deliver the marketing campaign:

  Follow through with delivery of the agreed marketing campaign

The "external view" of the project is the one that the manufacturing company has: "Create a marketing campaign to increase sales of product X by 15% without reducing the sales price."

The project deliverables, or internal view of the project would include:

- Market research results
- Market analysis results
- Create market campaign
- Marketing campaign sign-off
- Delivered campaign

Note that the internal view (deliverables) and the external view (goals) do not match.

The project team within the marketing company will be able to show that each of the internal deliverables has been successfully completed. However, completing these deliverables does not necessarily guarantee that the desired 15% increase in sales will be achieved.

Of course, it is vital that the internal view of the project will actually deliver the results and goals defined in the external view of the project. To help ensure that this happens, it is important that the external view is known and understood by the complete project team.

Project Management Theory

The project sponsor remains ultimately responsible for ensuring that the agreed project goals and requirements (external project view) are met. The project manager has the task of ensuring that the deliverables are completed successfully. The project manager will be expected to have the project goals in focus and to inform the project sponsor if there are any concerns that the deliverables will be insufficient to meet the overall project goals.

Project Management Theory

IDENTIFY THE RESOURCES REQUIRED TO DELIVER THE PROJECT DELIVERABLES

Split the Deliverables into Work Packages

Each agreed project deliverable is likely to require the combined effort of people from several different skill areas for it to be completed. Therefore, to co-ordinate the work as efficiently as possible, the deliverables need to be split into smaller work packages, each of which can be given to a single skill area to complete. The task(s) described in a work package need to be clearly understood by the person or team who is expected to deliver the results of the work package.

The project manager has the task of assigning the right work package to the right expert or team of experts and ensuring that each work package completes on time and within budget.

Using a Work Breakdown Structure (WBS) is an excellent method of breaking down large tasks into smaller work packages that can be completed by individuals or specialist teams. Refer to page 273 for a more detailed description of how to create a WBS. Using a WBS to decompose the deliverables helps to ensure that tasks do not get missed and provides a complete overview of how the work packages fit together to provide the project deliverables.

Estimate the Time and Resources Required to Complete the Project

To enable the project sponsor to decide on behalf of the organization if the project would be profitable or not, the project manager will need to provide a reasonably accurate business case. One essential part of the business case will be an estimation of the time and resources required to complete the project successfully. Resources in this case will include people, materials, available budget and the usage of machinery or workspace. These values can be expressed in monetary terms and are considered to be the project costs.

The more accurate the estimate of the time and resources required to complete the project successfully, the lower the risk to the organization will be. A lower risk makes it easier for the project sponsor to commit to the execution phase of the project.

The section *Estimating Techniques* in *Part V Tools* on page 280 contains information on a number of different methods of estimating the time and resources required to complete a project or a work package.

Project Management Theory

Confirm that the Required Resources would be Available to the Project

Before being able to approve the project, the project sponsor will need to know not only which resources are required to complete the project, but also whether or not the required resources would be available.

The resource estimation step, which occurred previously, will have identified the resources required. Now it is necessary to confirm that the organization is able to make the required resources available. Are the people with the required skills available? Is sufficient budget available? Is the required machinery and space available for the project to use?

Since the organization probably does not have resources that are lying around unused, this may turn into a question of priority. Is it beneficial to the organization to reallocate the required resources from their current tasks to this project? If the answer is yes, then the required resources are likely to be reassigned to the project.

If the required resources are not available, or cannot be made available, then the project has no chance of success and the project should not progress beyond this planning phase.

CREATE THE PROJECT PLAN

Generally, when people talk about the project plan, they are normally referring to the project delivery schedule. The project's delivery schedule states when each work package is due to be completed. It may include a number of milestones that could be used to communicate the progress made by the project team to the project's major stakeholders. However, the project delivery schedule is only one component of "the project plan".

The project plan is a collection of all the plans being used to manage the project. Some project management methodologies require quite a large number of plans to be included in the project plan: Procurement plan, training plan, change management plan, configuration management plan, requirements management plan, process improvement plan, etc. Except for very large projects, which require several hundred people committed over several years, most of these plans add little value to the project management process. The plans that create real value to the project management process are:

- The delivery schedule
- The resource plan
- The communications plan
- The risk mitigation plan (optional)

These are described below:

Project Management Theory

The Delivery Schedule

The delivery schedule states when each work package and each deliverable is expected to start and finish. Generally speaking, it is also a very useful tool for communicating the progress made on the project.

The resource plan and the delivery schedule are closely linked to each other. No delivery schedule will be reliable unless it has been confirmed that the resources required to complete the project will be available when they are needed.

Refer to *Project Schedule* on page 294 in *Part V Tools* for more details on tools that could be used for creating a delivery schedule.

The Resource Plan

The resource plan describes which resources are required at which time.

The resources required for a project change as a project progresses. Different tasks require different resources. In general, the initiation and planning phase of a project generally require only a small number of people and very few other resources. Once the project progresses into the execution phase, the amount of resources being used increases dramatically. As the project completes most of the work and moves towards completion and closure, the

Project Management Theory

resource usage starts to drop again. Refer to the diagram below for a typical example of resource usage over time.

Resource Usage over Time

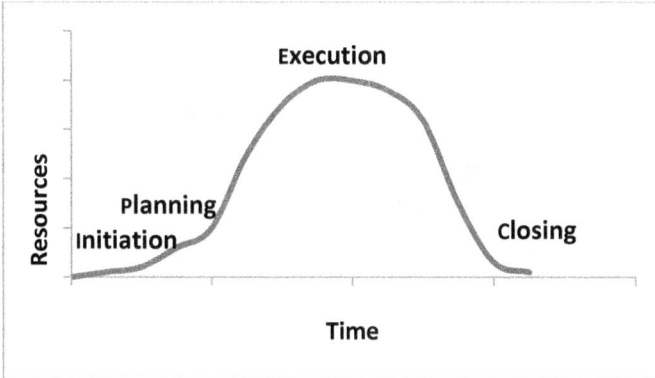

As the graph above shows, resource planning is mainly required to support the execution phase of the project, because this is the phase where resources are most intensively used. Some machinery may only be required for one or two particular work packages. People from one particular skill area may be required to support the project intensely for a short time and then not be required for the rest of the project. Other people, workspaces, or machinery may be required continuously throughout the project.

In any project, members of the project team will need to make themselves available at specific times so that the work packages can be completed according to the agreed project schedule. There will however, be dates when the

Project Management Theory

members of the project team are unavailable: vacation, critical operational tasks, commitments to other projects, etc.

The resource plan describes when the required resources are available (or rather, in this phase of the project, can be made available) to the project. Since any work package is dependent upon the required resources being available at the right time, this information needs to be fed back into the project schedule. It may take a couple of revisions of the project schedule and the resource plan until both can be finalized.

The Communication Plan

Effective communication between all the interested parties will play a vital role in the success of the project. Considering the sheer volume of communication that needs to happen for even a small- or medium-sized project to complete successfully, it is important to plan communications for them to be effective.

The types of communication required include:

- The project manager will need to have regular contact with their project team to gather status and distribute work

- The project team will need to exchange information regularly between the different skill areas
- The project manager and the project sponsor will need to report progress and maintain the support of stakeholders who are not part of the project team
- All the stakeholders in the project will need to know what the status is and what the next steps are

A communication plan describes how information will flow regularly within the project. In essence, it states two things:

- Which meetings will be held, how often they will be held, and who should attend them
- Which reports will need to be created, how often they will be created, and who they will be sent to

For some projects, there may also be a need to communicate progress to a much wider audience than a typical meeting structure can cope with. In this case, some sort of broadcast communication, such a newsletter, may be required to keep everyone with a justified interest informed.

Project Management Theory

The Risk Mitigation Plan

Before we can talk about the risk mitigation plan itself, we need to talk briefly about risk management.

The number of ways in which a project can go wrong is impressively large. Risk management has the goal of anticipating what might go wrong during execution and taking action to reduce the chance that these things actually will happen. More specifically, risk management has the goals of reducing unplanned costs associated with delivering the project results to a minimum and of ensuring that nothing goes wrong with the project in a way that would cause damage to the organization.

The first step towards managing risk is to identify the different risks associated with the project. Use input from the entire project planning team to ensure that as many risks as possible are identified and recorded.

The next step is to quantify the risk to the organization. Two factors are important here:

1. How likely is it that the risk will become reality?
2. What is the impact to the project, and the organization, if the risk should become reality?

An assessment based on these two factors provides a good guideline on the amount of effort that should be invested into a risk mitigation strategy for each individual risk. Risk mitigation strategies have the task of reducing or avoiding the risk.

Once all the risk mitigation strategies have been decided, these are collected together into the risk mitigation plan so that the risks can be managed during project execution.

So the risk mitigation plan includes:

- A list of the risks which the project manager has decided are significant enough that they need to be actively managed (if any)
- A statement regarding the impact to the project (or organization) if the risk occurs
- A statement of how likely it is that the risk will occur
- A statement detailing the actions which will be taken to either reduce the risk or to avoid it completely

Refer to *Chapter 23 Risk Management* in *Tools*, on page 309 for more detailed information on risk management.

CREATE THE DETAILED BUSINESS CASE

When deciding if the project should be completed or not, the project sponsor will want to know if the project would profitable for the organization. The detailed business plan will provide this information.

There are some projects that an organization is required to complete. There may be a requirement to obtain a certification required by the industry, or to conform to some new legislation. In these and similar instances, the business case reduces to: implement the project or stop doing business. Under these circumstances, a formal business case is probably not helpful to the project sponsor or the executive management team. This is, however, relatively rare and most projects will have a business case attached to them.

By this point in the planning phase, all the expected costs of completing the project should be known. Not only should the expected costs be known, the project planning team should also know if sufficient resources can be made available to the project and what the time line for delivery of the project results would be.

The project team will need to calculate the benefits to the organization of completing the project. In most cases where a formal business case is required, the benefit to the organization is generally well understood because there is a clear financial benefit if the project is completed. In some cases though, the benefit to the organization is not so clearly defined. For example, it may be very difficult to predict the financial benefit to the organization of a quality improvement program. The impact of the improved quality in terms of increased customer satisfaction and improved reputation may be difficult to measure directly, even though the direct savings related to a reduced failure rate can be calculated clearly.

A formal business case needs to be created which shows the costs to the organization of completing the project, and compares these costs with the expected benefit to the organization of completing the project.

If the formal business case shows that it is in the best interest of the organization to complete the project, then the project sponsor is highly likely to commit the resources to execute the project. If the business case shows that it would not be profitable or advantageous to the organization to complete the project, then the project requirements and deliverables will need to be reassessed or the entire project cancelled.

The detailed business case will need to be approved by the project sponsor before the project can progress to the execution and monitoring phase. Approval could be gathered during a business case review meeting or as part of the formal decision to commit to the project.

Project Management Theory

CREATE THE SCOPE STATEMENT

The scope statement is one of the most important project documents. The project scope statement is required by the project manager and the project sponsor. It defines what the project is expected to deliver and what resources the organization will need to make available for the project manager to be able to deliver the expected project results.

To ensure completeness, the scope statement summarizes a lot of the information that was discovered during the planning phase of the project. The most important information to be included in the scope statement is:

- An outline of the overall goal of the project (external project view)
- A summary of the expected deliverables (internal project view)
- A statement regarding when the deliverables are expected to be available
- A summary of the resources which will be made available to the project manager

When the project sponsor agrees to the project scope statement, then they agree, on behalf of the organization, to make all the resources documented in the project scope statement available to the project manager. When the project manager agrees to the project scope, they agree to accept the task to deliver the described results within the described time frame using the described resources.

Any changes to the scope statement as the project progresses will need to be approved by both the project sponsor and the project manager.

Project Management Theory

FORMALLY COMMIT TO THE PROJECT

With the information available in the scope statement and the supporting planning information, the organization knows as much as it is possible to know about the project without actually starting the execution phase of the project.

Based on the available information, the project sponsor will assess if it is in the best interest of the organization to execute the project. Then the project sponsor will make a formal decision and either approve the project and commit all the necessary resources required for the completion of the project, or stop the project from progressing further.

Project Management Theory

CHAPTER 11.

EXECUTION & MONITORING

The execution part of the execution and monitoring phase is where the project results are created. In other words, this is where the work gets done.

The monitoring part of the execution and monitoring phase has the task of ensuring that the project is progressing according to the plan. It provides a regular check: Is it still reasonable to believe that the project results will be delivered on time, within budget, and to the expected level of quality?

Implicit in the monitoring task is the expectation that if the work is currently not progressing according to the plan, then the project manager will implement some form of change to bring the project back onto track.

The steps involved in the execution and monitoring phase include:

- Formally starting the project
- Execution
  This is a cyclical process and includes these steps:
  - Distribute work
  - Monitor progress

Project Management Theory

- Includes reporting and communication
- Cost control
- Risk management
  - Plan changes
  - Implement changes
- Complete the execution phase

Project Management Theory

FORMALLY STARTING THE EXECUTION AND MONITORING PHASE: THE KICK-OFF MEETING

Ideally, the execution and monitoring phase of the project is started with a formal kick-off meeting. The main purpose of this meeting is to inform everyone involved in the project that the project is starting. Each member of the project team will need to understand their own tasks and how these tasks fit together to create the final project results. Equally important, the project team will be introduced to each other so that each team member knows who they will be working with and what the other team member's tasks will be.

If a kick-off meeting is not possible, then some other method (E-Mail, telephone call) will be necessary to inform each of the team members about the project and their role in it.

Project Management Theory

EXECUTION

The central process related to the project execution is cyclic and is under the control of the project manager.

Execution Process Cycle Summary

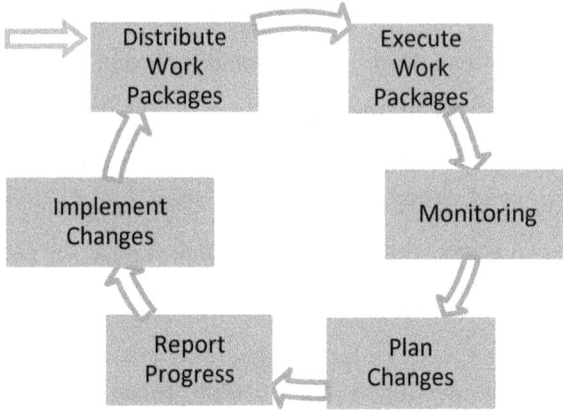

Distribute Work Packages

The execution process starts directly after the kick-off meeting with the initial distribution of work packages that have no prerequisites. As the project progresses, work packages will be completed. Some of these will have completed the prerequisites that were necessary to allow other work packages to start. Any work packages which have had all their prerequisites fulfilled can be distributed to the project team for them to start work on.

Execute Work Packages

The experts in the project team complete the tasks defined in the work packages and provide regular feedback on the progress being made.

Monitoring

The project manager will need to keep track of the overall project progress, as well as the progress of the individual work packages. This can normally be achieved in the regular progress meetings.

The main factors which will need to be monitored regularly are:

- Progress Management: Are the work packages being completed according to the schedule?
- Cost Management: Is the available remaining budget sufficient to complete the remaining tasks?
- Quality Management: Is the work being completed to the expected quality standards
- Risk Management: Are the risk mitigation strategies working? Have any new risks been identified? Can any risks now be removed?

Project Management Theory

Project Management Theory

Progress Management

The main task of progress management is to check that the work packages are being completed on schedule. If the work packages are not being completed on schedule, then the reason why needs to be identified and changes made so that work package completion get back on schedule.

If a work package is delayed for some reason, then it is especially useful to know if that work package is on the critical path or not. (See the box below for an explanation of the project critical path.) If the work package is on the critical path then the project manager will need to take immediate action to avoid delaying the final project delivery. However, if the work package is not on the critical path then there will be some leeway to allow the work package to slip.

Project Critical Path

A work package is on the project's critical path if any delay (no matter how small) to the work package will cause a delay to the final project delivery.

The critical path of a project describes the shortest time in which the project can be completed.

A project has a number of work packages that need to be finished before the project can complete. Some work packages will need to be completed consecutively. Some

---

can run in parallel. This can lead to a project having two or more streams of work active at the same time. The work in one stream of the project may require less time to complete than the work in other streams. The stream that will take the longest time to complete defines the shortest time in which the project could be completed. This stream is referred to as the critical path for the project. If any of the work packages on the critical path are delayed, then the final project completion will also be delayed.

Refer to *Project Schedule* in *Part V Tools* on page 294 for more details on network diagrams. Network diagrams help to improve understanding of the critical path concept by putting it into a visual form.

Project Management Theory

Cost Management

The main question to be answered by cost management is, will the remaining budget be sufficient to complete the remaining tasks?

Any project has costs associated with it. Subtracting the costs to date from the original project budget will show the current available budget. The expected cost to complete the work that is still outstanding should be available from the planning phase. If planning information can no longer be considered reliable, then the project manager will need to organize an updated cost estimate.

If the available budget is insufficient to complete the remaining work, then the project manager will need to inform the project sponsor immediately. In parallel, they need to investigate if the project team can resolve the situation without asking for extra budget.

Refer to *Cost Management*, on page 350 for more details on cost management tools and techniques.

Quality Management

Quality management has the task of ensuring that the results being produced by the project will meet the quality expectations of the person who receives the project results.

Quality measures were agreed to during planning. Therefore, the main task in quality management is to ensure that the project results being produced can be shown to meet these quality standards.

Risk Management

The project risks need to be reviewed regularly. As the project work completes, some risks will cease to exist and can be struck from the risk register. The project team may also identify new risks, which were not apparent during planning. These newly identified risks will need to be added to the project risk register and a risk mitigation plan implemented if appropriate.

Part V Tools, Risk Management, on page 309 covers risk management in detail.

Plan Changes

There are two main sources of project changes: Internal and External.

Project Internal Changes

Internal changes are changes that have come from the project team. The most likely cause is that one of the monitoring tasks described above has identified an issue that requires a project change in order to resolve it. It is also possible that one of the team members has identified an opportunity to improve the project results or the way the project results are being produced.

If the project team discovers an improvement to the project, then the project team will want to take advantage of this opportunity. If the discovery is significant enough, then everyone in the organization who can take advantage of it will need to be informed.

Dealing with issues is part of the daily work of a project manager. Generally speaking, the earlier issues are identified, the easier they are to resolve without impacting the project significantly. This means that a reporting structure needs to be in place so that the project manager is informed of issues as soon as they occur. To support the

Project Management Theory

reporting structure, there also needs to be an organizational culture in place that encourages the project team to bring issues to the notice of the project manager so they can be discussed constructively.

If the project manager can solve the issue within the scope of the resources and authorizations given to them by the project sponsor, then the project manager will be expected to solve the issue.

If this is not possible, then the project manager will need to discuss the issue with the project sponsor before proceeding. The project sponsor may decide to expand the remit of the project manager so that they can solve the issue directly. Alternatively, the project sponsor might decide to resolve the issue themselves or provide some kind of additional support for the project team.

Scope Change

Scope changes are normally requested by the project sponsor or the receiver of the project results and not the project team. Changes to the scope of the project after planning has been completed may become necessary for any number or reasons:

- When the first project results become available it may become obvious that a change of scope is necessary to fulfill the overall project goal

Project Management Theory

- Changes within the organization or in the organization's operational environment may force a review of the overall project goals and scope
- The customer receiving the project's results may have decided that a scope change is necessary for them to receive the full benefits of the results which the project intends to deliver
- Legislation may change during the delivery of a project, forcing the organization to make some changes
- It may be necessary to agree to a new completion date

A change in scope will lead to the project being either partially or completely re-planned. It is likely that the overall project budget and other required resources will need to change.

Any such change needs to be approved by both the project sponsor and the project manager before it is implemented. The project sponsor is responsible for providing the budget and other resources required to deliver the project deliverables and goals and will need to approve the change. The project manager is responsible for delivery of the project results. If the results required are changed, then the project manager will need to confirm that the changed scope can be completed according to the updated plan.

Project Management Theory

Change planning

Each change to the project will affect at least one part of the project plan. This could be the resource plan, the project schedule, the communication plan, or the risk mitigation plan. Change planning is similar to the work done during the planning phase of the project, except it is just done for a single part instead of for the whole thing.

If the change is an internal one, and does not affect the project scope, the project manager will be able to implement it directly.

If the change affects the project scope, then the project manager and the project sponsor will need to agree to the change together.

Report Progress

The project manager will need to prepare reports to inform the project sponsor, and any other important stakeholders, about the overall progress. These reports should be delivered as agreed in the project communication plan.

Reporting is placed before Implement Changes because it is normally necessary to report the progress and explain a need for the project change before agreement to implement the change can be given.

Project Management Theory

Implement Changes

Once the change has been agreed to, the project manager will need to implement it. This will involve making the team aware of how the project plan has been changed and asking them to work according to the updated plan.

Regular monitoring, as part of the normal execution and monitoring cycle, will confirm that the change has been put into place properly.

Project Management Theory

COMPLETING EXECUTION

Eventually, all the work packages that had been planned will have completed. No further repetitions of the execution and monitoring cycle will be necessary, because there is nothing left to do.

Once all the planned tasks from the execution and monitoring phase have been completed, the project will move automatically into the closing phase.

Before moving into the formal closing phase, the project manager should confirm that:

- all the work packages are complete and meet the agreed quality expectations
- all the expected deliverables are complete and meet the agreed quality expectations
- the overall project goals have been achieved

Project Management Theory

CHAPTER 12.

CLOSING

All the deliverables have been completed and the goals of the project have been met. Now is the time for the project to be closed down. The closing phase contains all the actions that are necessary for the project to be formally recognized as being completed.

The tasks to be performed include:

- Formal handover of the project results to the project sponsor
- Gather the lessons learned during the project
- Formally close the project
  - Communicate project completion to all stakeholders
  - Release the people and other remaining resources from the project

Project Management Theory

FORMAL HANDOVER OF THE PROJECT RESULTS TO THE PROJECT SPONSOR

Formal handover of the project results to the project sponsor marks the end of the project execution and monitoring phase and the start of the closing phase of the project.

Where possible, the actual project results are handed over directly to the project sponsor. Depending on the nature of the project, it may be inappropriate to hand over the actual product result. Where the actual project results cannot be directly handed over, the supporting documentation would be delivered to provide evidence that the work has been completed and the desired results have been achieved.

The project sponsor will formally accept the results and in turn hand over the project results to the organization or to the customer as appropriate.

Project Management Theory

LESSONS LEARNED

To ensure that the knowledge which was created during the project lifecycle is not lost as the project team disperses back to their normal line tasks, it is important that that the lessons which the project team learned are captured and made available to the organization for future use.

This knowledge could be captured in a project completion report, in a knowledge base, and/or in set of improved processes to be implemented in the organization. At the very least, the knowledge should be captured by the PMO (Project Management Office) and made available to anyone who attempts to perform a similar project in the future. The knowledge retained by the PMO should include details on what went well (things to be repeated) and what went badly (things to be avoided) – preferably with pointers on how to do things better in the future.

Project Management Theory

FORMAL CLOSURE

Once the project team has held a lessons learned session and captured the knowledge gained during the project, and the project sponsor has accepted the project results, the project can be formally closed.

Formal closure includes checking that all the project information is complete, and finalizing any administrative tasks related to the project.

All stakeholders in the project will need to be informed that the project has now completed. Typically, either the project manager or the project sponsor will prepare a short message to the organization to explain that the project has completed and what the resultant benefits to the organization are.

Any open costs will need to be booked against the project cost code and the cost code closed.

The project team will need to be released from the project by the project manager so that they can return to their normal line work. In turn, the project manager will need to be released from the project by the project sponsor.

Part IV

Project Management Practice

CHAPTER 13.

INTRODUCTION TO PROJECT MANAGEMENT PRACTICE

The focus in Stripped Down Project Management is on the most important steps that a project needs to complete if it is to complete successfully. Each step in the process produces a clear result that either is needed in a later stage in the project, or directly supports project progress.

This part of this book has been written as a step-by-step guide on how to complete a project. This approach has proven itself to be very effective and helpful to the project managers that I have coached or trained. It has helped them to stay focused on the most important tasks to be completed during each phase of the project. In turn, this has helped them to deliver the project successfully with as little project overhead as possible.

The methodology is presented here as a "best practice" approach and does not delve too deeply into the 1001 variations that may be necessary to meet specific circumstances in real life. In practice, project managers have been able to adapt the approach here quite easily to fit the special circumstances of their project or working environment.

While working on a project, it is important to recognize that a project is unlikely to run exactly as it was planned. Some tasks will be completed sooner or with less effort than expected, some tasks will take longer. As a project manager, is important to keep track of the overall progress and take steps to ensure that the overall goals can be achieved on time and within budget.

This practice part can be read independently of *Part III Project Management Theory*. However, the practice and theory parts of this book are intended to complement one another.

To keep the main text easy to follow, and to minimize repeated information in both the theory and practice parts of the book, detailed discussion of project management tools has been moved to *Part V Tools*, which starts on page 253.

Project Management Practice

CHAPTER 14.

INITIATION

Project initiation includes completing all the tasks that are necessary to create the project. The overall goal of the initiation phase is to prepare everything so that the planning team can start work once the project sponsor has given the go ahead for the project to move into the planning phase.

It is the job of the project sponsor to define clearly what the project is intended to achieve and, often equally as important, what it will not achieve. In other words, the scope of the project needs to be set.

The Project Sponsor's tasks during initiation are:

- To ensure that the projects goals or requirements (the external view of the project) will be clearly understood by everyone who will work on the project.
  Clearly understood means that the goals are defined specifically enough so that the specialists involved in the project planning and execution will understand unambiguously what the project team is expected to deliver
- Assign a project manager with the necessary skills to complete the project

Project Management Practice

- Define how quality will be measured
- Create an outline business case for the project
- Identify the major project stakeholders
- Make the decision to commit the resources necessary to perform the detailed project planning
- Perform the administrative tasks necessary to start the project within the organization

In practice, many project sponsors simply do not have the time to complete all these tasks themselves. The project manager will need to complete any tasks that the project sponsor was unable to finish. For this, and other reasons, it is definitely recommended to involve the project manager in the initiation phase as early as possible. Some advantages of having the project manager on board early are:

- The project manager, who will be responsible for running the project, will have an opportunity to shape the project
- The project manager can give their input on how the project should be structured and what the major deliverables should be
- The project manager will have the opportunity for direct contact with the people who are requesting the project results

Project Management Practice

- By being involved in the conception phase, the general background and overall goals of the project are clearly understood by the project manager right from the start
- The project manager can support the project sponsor with their initiation tasks

Remember that the project sponsor has ultimate responsibility for delivery of the project results. The initiation phase is the project sponsor's best chance to ensure that the project is correctly set up and everyone is working towards a common goal. Investing a little extra time now to provide the best possible conditions for the project to succeed is likely to save considerable time and effort later on.

Completion of the initiation phase is marked by the completion of any administrative tasks that are required within the organization to recognize the project, and the formal decision to commit the resources necessary to plan the project.

Project Management Practice

CLARIFY THE GOALS OF THE PROJECT

Clearly defining the goal of the project is often one of the more difficult tasks that a project sponsor has. At the start of the initiation phase, there is typically only a vague idea of what needs to be done. In some cases, there may be a clearly defined goal, but with no idea of how the goal is to be achieved. In other cases, the goal itself is not clearly defined enough for work to start. In either case, work will need to be done to refine the project scope.

When defining the scope, the project sponsor needs to provide an appropriate level of detail.

If the project sponsor defines a very tight scope, then there is no room left for the project team to develop creative solutions or to take advantage of discovered opportunities.

Conversely, if the goal is too loosely defined, or the scope of the project too wide, then there exists the risk that the project manager may go off at a tangent wasting time and resources until such time as the situation is identified and rectified. In extreme cases, the overall project goal may not be attained because the project manager and project team have misunderstood what the project was expected to achieve.

Project Management Practice

The solution is normally to define a scope and discuss it with the project manager. Then, during the regular steering board meetings, check that the project is still heading in the right direction.

Important factors in deciding the level of detail in which the project goal needs to be defined and the frequency of meetings that are required to ensure that the project remains on track are:

- How well the project sponsor knows the project manager
- How well the project manager understands the environmental factors in which the organization operates
- How experienced the project manager is with this type of project.

Another useful guideline is that the project goals should state *what* is to be achieved, but *not* how it should be achieved. Stating how the work should be achieved generally limits the project team to much.

In an ideal world, a project sponsor should write a clear statement of the project goals explaining exactly what the project is expected to achieve. In practice, most project sponsors simply do not have the time to do so. Therefore, if the project sponsor does not have time to write down the goals of the project with sufficient clarity themselves, they need to ask the project manager to do this on their behalf. In this case, the project sponsor will need to review the project goals with the project manager, ensure that they have been properly understood, and then approve them.

If the project goals need to be refined later on as the project progresses and better information becomes available, then this is easily explained and is likely to be accepted by all the major stakeholders without much discussion. Late changes to the project caused by misunderstandings between the project sponsor and the project manager are likely to be seen as an avoidable waste of resources and justly criticized.

Project Management Practice

SELECT THE PROJECT MANAGER

The project manager will manage the project on behalf of the project sponsor. An ideal candidate will be someone who understands the task in detail, understands the environmental factors under which the organization operates, and has a good understanding of the relevant processes inside the organization. It should be someone the project sponsor is comfortable working with, who has the skills which the project requires, and be someone who the project sponsor is happy to have representing them.

Since this is a new undertaking for the organization, the necessary skills may not be available within the organization. In this case, the project sponsor may prefer to arrange for an external project manager who has run similar projects successfully for other organizations.

An external candidate will most likely not be as knowledgeable as an internal candidate would have been of the organization's internal processes and the environment in which the organization operates. The project sponsor may need to plan for additional support for an external project manager to fill this knowledge gap.

An internal project manager may be new to the task at hand, but is likely to understand the organization and the relevant environmental factors under which the organization operates better than an external project

Project Management Practice

manager would. Using an internal project manager has the additional benefit of retaining experience gained and knowledge learned during the project within the organization.

Regardless of the path chosen, an ideal candidate for the post of project manager may not be available and the project sponsor will need to select the best possible project manager from the available candidates. Additional support may need to be provided (in terms of personal support or extending the project team) to make up for any gaps which the project manager has in knowledge, skill, or experience.

Project Management Practice

DEFINE QUALITY MEASURES

Failure to define quality measures can cause huge problems when the completed project results are handed over to the project sponsor or the receiver of the project results.

Exceeding quality expectations may be interpreted to mean that the project could have been completed either quicker or at a lower cost. Not meeting quality expectations may lead to the project deliverables not being accepted as fit for the desired purpose, necessitating a complete rework of some or all of the project deliverables.

To avoid these kinds of issues, quality needs to be discussed during initiation, or at the very latest during planning. The biggest difficulty here is that quality is often subjective. To avoid conflicting understandings of what "quality" means in the context of a project, it is important to make an attempt to define "quality" in terms that can be measured objectively.

Quality is often understood to be a statement regarding the number of defects that a final product may have. In any instance where large scale repetition is involved (manufacturing, services), then the quality can be stated as being the number of times per (million / thousand) that

Project Management Practice

the manufactured part was defective or the service did not produce the expected result.

For example, for a television manufacturer, quality measures could be the number of televisions which:

1. do not work when the customer first buys the product
2. fail during the guarantee period

An alternative interpretation of quality can also be used to express by how far the minimum requirements to complete the work were exceeded. For example, a construction company may build a building using materials and design which exceed the minimum standards required by the local building regulations or customer expectations.

Quality measures here could be:

1. The energy efficiency of the building
2. The amount outside noise is reduced when inside the building
3. How secure the building is against unauthorized entry
4. The value of the interior fittings

By finding and agreeing to objective measures of quality as early as possible in the project, risk of disagreement

Project Management Practice

regarding the delivered project quality in the final phases of the project, when it costs the most to resolve, is minimized.

CREATE AN OUTLINE BUSINESS CASE

Normally, a project will have a business case related to it. The project will only be considered for execution if the benefit to the organization is greater than the cost of completing the project.

During the initiation phase of the project, only a basic understanding of the business case parameters will be available to the project sponsor because the full costs of the project to the organization will not be known until the planning phase has been completed. Despite this, if the project sponsor makes the outline of the business case available to the planning team, it will help them to produce a plan that is in line with the organization's overall goals and the project sponsor's expectations.

If the planning phase is going to require considerable time and resources to complete, then it is useful at this phase to get a rough estimate of the total required budget so that the project feasibility can be confirmed before committing the resources required to complete a more detailed planning.

The project sponsor (or the project manager if one is already assigned to the project) will need to contact the relevant experts, or their line managers, and ask for a rough estimate of the resources required to complete the work necessary to achieve the project's goals. The

Project Management Practice

estimates will be based on past experience / best guesses and should be expected to have a considerable range of error.

Once the outline business case has been created, the project sponsor needs to review it. If the business case is not compelling then either the project goals need to be reviewed, or the intended method of project implementation needs to be reviewed. If improvements can be identified which would improve the business case, then these improvements should be made now.

If assumptions are made in the outline business case, it is important that these be noted. They will be required later on during the detailed planning.

IDENTIFY THE PROJECT STAKEHOLDERS

In project management theory, stakeholders include anyone who has a legitimate reason to be interested in the project. This is a very broad definition which quite famously also includes the organization's competitors. In some special cases, it may be useful to consider such a broad set of stakeholders. For the vast majority of projects however, this definition is simply too broad to be useful.

In the interest of reducing workload, Stripped Down Project Management recommends a shorter list of stakeholders. For most projects, it is more useful to consider the project stakeholders to be anyone who is directly involved with the project and anyone who needs to be kept regularly informed of the status of the project.

A reasonable starting point for the list of project stakeholders would be:

- The project sponsor
- The people who will receive the project results
- Everyone in the project team (add these as they become known)
- People who are not part of the project team, but have the ability to influence the project significantly
- Any necessary contacts, such as suppliers

Project Management Practice

> **Note:**
>
> This stakeholder list will need to be managed and maintained during the project lifecycle. It is to be expected that at least some changes to the project team will occur over the duration of the project.

The stakeholder list is a useful list for the project manager. They will need it later for:

- Ensuring that regular contact is maintained with all members of the project team
- Ensuring reports are sent to all the people who need to be kept informed of the status of the project
- Stakeholder management

Stakeholder management is basically a fancy term for ensuring that all the influential stakeholders in the project are informed of the progress of the project and are kept happy. This is done so that they continue to support (or at least, do not obstruct) the project. This may sound like a trivial task, but the larger, more complex, or riskier that a project is, the greater the importance of actively managing the project's stakeholders becomes.

DECISION: COMMIT THE RESOURCES FOR PROJECT PLANNING

Once the project sponsor has sufficient information available to make an informed decision regarding whether or not it is in the best interests of the organization to commit the necessary resources to plan the project in detail, then they should do so. This will enable the project to move from the initiation phase into the planning phase.

To make an informed decision, the project sponsor will need to have the following available:

- A clearly defined project goal which describes what the project is intended to achieve
- A capable project manager
- Knowledge of which people need to be included in the project planning team
- An outline business case which is compelling enough to justify committing the resources necessary to plan the project in detail

In addition to the points above, the project sponsor will need to take into account how well the project fits into the organization's environment and strategic goals.

After consideration of all these factors, the project sponsor should be in a position to make the decision whether to continue with the project and commit the resources

Project Management Practice

necessary to plan the project in detail, or to stop the project.

PERFORM THE ADMINISTRATIVE ACTIONS REQUIRED TO INITIATE THE PROJECT

When the decision has been made to continue with the project and move to the planning phase, there will typically be a few administrative tasks that are required so that the project is recognized by the organization. Completing these administrative tasks will inform the rest of the organization that the project exists and is now moving into the planning phase.

Each organization will have their procedures for formally starting a project. The steps described below make the assumption that there is a central PMO in place as described in the chapter *The PMO (Project Management Office)* on page 31.

Inform the PMO of the Project

The PMO will need to be informed of the project and the current status: initiation completed; planning is due to start almost immediately. Typically, the PMO will assign the project a number or code and make a central documentation repository available to the project team.

If the PMO has set standards for project management, project progress reporting templates, risk management, and so on, then this information will be given to the project manager if they do not already have it.

Project Management Practice

Ensure Cost Tracking is in Place

Information regarding how much a particular project costs is valuable information. This information can be used to show empirically that the organization is improving at project delivery as well as providing a baseline that can be used to improve cost estimates for similar projects in the future.

Ideally, the organization already has some cost tracking system in place that is used to book the time and costs for work performed on different projects. If this is the case, the project sponsor will request a project cost code so that all the project related costs can be booked against the relevant cost code.

CHAPTER 15.

PROJECT PLANNING

The planning phase takes the results from the initiation phase and uses them to create a detailed plan for project execution.

During the initiation phase, the project sponsor had the clear lead. With the close of the initiation phase, and the formal commitment from the project sponsor to move to the planning phase, the lead is passed over to the project manager. The project manager will manage the planning team with the aim of creating a detailed project plan for the project.

The overall goal of the project planning phase is to enable a "go / no go" decision for the execution of the project to be made by the project sponsor. In order for the project sponsor to make the decision to commit all the necessary resources required to complete the project, the project sponsor will need to know what the project deliverables will be, which resources will need to be committed, and when the project is expected to complete. All these details are brought together in summary form a single document referred to as the scope statement.

Assuming that the project sponsor approves the project for execution, then the project manager will require

Project Management Practice

accurate project planning information to manage the project during the execution phase. Therefore, this work has a dual function:

- To enable the project sponsor to make the decision to commit to project execution
- To provide the project manager with a plan which can be used to manage the project

Project Planning Accuracy

The project will provide something that is new to the organization. Therefore, even the most careful planning is likely to have some inaccuracies. The organization may be able to take advantage of some unexpected opportunities and (more likely) some things may cost more or take longer than initially expected.

How accurate the plan is expected to be will be dependent upon how much experience the organization has at performing comparable projects in the past and what level of risk is considered to be acceptable within the organization.

In some organizations, the project sponsor will deliberately set a tight budget to spur project managers on to achieve as much as possible using as few resources as possible. In other organizations, the project sponsor will prefer to provide a more generous budget but will not

Project Management Practice

accept a budget increase except in truly exceptional circumstances.

Be sure to understand these environmental factors for your organization and prepare your plan accordingly.

The tasks in the planning phase of the project are:

- Evaluate the project goals
- Define the deliverables
- Estimate the time and resources required to complete the project
- Create the project plan
- Complete a risk assessment
- Provide a detailed business case
- Create the scope statement
- Decision: Commit the resources required to execute the project, or stop the project

EVALUATE THE PROJECT GOALS

The project manager will need to review the supplied project goals to ensure that the project is clearly understood. If any points are unclear or inconsistent, then the project manager will need to seek clarification from the project sponsor. If the project manager was involved during the initiation phase of the project, then the project manager should already be aware of these goals. Even so, a review is a worthwhile exercise.

The project manager will need to ensure that a copy of the currently known project goals (requirements, deliverables, etc.) is stored in the central project repository provided by the PMO for this project. This will need to be available later in the event of a disagreement about what the project was intended to achieve.

Do not underestimate the importance of getting the project goals correct. An amazing number of projects have failed spectacularly due to a misunderstanding of the project's goals.

DEFINE THE DELIVERABLES

Often, project goals are defined in the form of business requirements or customer requirements. The project results will need to meet these requirements. Typically, these requirements are written in terms that make sense to the receiver of the project results and the project sponsor. They create the external view of what the project will deliver.

It is, however, highly unlikely that the project goals will be defined in terms of the particular tasks that the project team will actually deliver. The project planning team will need to create a set of deliverables which, when taken together, will achieve the stated project goals. (Refer to *Chapter 10 Planning* on page 78 for more details on the difference between the internal and external view of the project.)

The deliverable items will need to be clearly understood by the technical experts working on the project team during the execution phase. These items are normally quite similar to the work which the expert or team of experts performs regularly.

When defining the deliverables, it is important to ensure that they are defined in such a way so that it is clear to everyone involved when the deliverable is complete. For example:

Project Management Practice

- If you are running a quality improvement project, do not say "improve ..." Set a definite goal.

- If you are developing a next generation product, do not say "develop next generation of ..." Define clearly which features will be added.

- If you are creating a product or service for a specific customer, take the time to detail what the major components of the product or service will be. Define, for each major component, what will be required so that the overall product or service fits the customer's expectations.

During closure phase, it will be important that all the major stakeholders for the project are able to agree that the expected project results have actually been delivered. If this is not done, then no matter how good or bad the results are, there is likely to discussion and dissatisfaction during the closure of the project.

Get confirmation from the project sponsor that the defined project deliverables will meet the project goals and requirements. If doubt or discrepancies exist, get them cleared up now to avoid wasting time and resources delivering the wrong results later.

Project Management Practice

Once the deliverables have been defined, store the agreed description of the deliverables in the central project repository provided by the PMO along with confirmation from the project sponsor that this is what the project should achieve.

Project Management Practice

ESTIMATE THE TIME AND RESOURCES REQUIRED TO COMPLETE THE PROJECT

An initial rough estimate of the time and resources required to complete the project may have been done during the initiation phase of the project.

Whether ballpark figures are available or not, now is the time to create a detailed and reliable estimate of the required resources. The project manager is responsible for ensuring the described deliverables are completed on time using the available resources. Therefore, it is important to get feedback from the project sponsor regarding what they consider to be an acceptable level of accuracy.

Before creating the time and resource estimates, review the goals and requirements documents and the description of the expected deliverables.

Estimation of the time and resources required to complete the project will be done in three steps:

- Split the deliverables into work packages
- Estimate the time and resources required to complete the work packages
- Confirm that the resources required to complete the work packages could be made available to the project within the expected time frame for project execution

Project Management Practice

Split the Deliverables into Work Packages

Each agreed deliverable will probably still be a relatively complex task requiring more than one skill area to complete. It is difficult to manage complex tasks like this because:

- It is difficult to be able to tell if the specialist teams are making the expected progress or if they are gradually falling behind schedule. Without intermediate control points, tracking progress against the schedule is difficult

- It is difficult to know when the each specialist team needs to be involved. This often creates a need to have all the specialists available all the time, which wastes resources

- It is difficult to demonstrate progress to the project sponsor and any other influential stakeholders. Without smaller tasks being completed regularly, the project report will show the same status for a long time. ("Working on Deliverable X".) This will leave the project sponsor concerned. They will see the project expenditure, but have no evidence of progress

To make the task of managing complex deliverables easier, it is helpful to split each of the deliverables into a set of smaller pieces of work called work packages. Each work package should ideally require only one expert or expert team, to complete the tasks included in it. This makes the dependencies between work packages transparent, allows the individual experts to be responsible for delivering "their" work packages, and reduces the level of complexity of each work package. A single work package should not take more than about 4 weeks to complete, ideally less. This helps the project manager to keep track of overall project progress and makes it easier to demonstrate progress to the project sponsor.

Using a Work Breakdown Structure (WBS) is an excellent method of decomposing large tasks into smaller work packages, each of which can be completed by individuals or specialist teams. Refer to *Work Breakdown Structure* on page 273 for a more detailed description of how to create a WBS. Using a WBS to decompose the deliverables helps to ensure that tasks do not get missed and provides a complete overview of how the work packages fit together to provide the project deliverables.

The project manager will need to work together with representatives from the relevant skill areas to define suitable work packages. In particular, the project manager will need to ensure that the content of each individual work is clearly understood and that one person feels responsible for delivering the work in that package.

Each work package will need:

- A short description of the work to be completed and the expected result
- The resources required to complete the work package. Refer to the next section for more details on estimating resources
- The expected start and end dates
- Any dependencies that this work package has on other work packages

Refer to *Work Package Template* on page 372 for an example of a work package template.

Estimate the Time and Resources Required to Complete the Work Packages

To enable the project sponsor to decide on behalf of the organization if the project would be profitable or not, a reasonably accurate estimation of the time and resources necessary to complete the project successfully will be needed. Resources in this sense will include people, materials, available budget, machinery, and work space.

Producing good estimates of how long a particular task will take is surprisingly difficult if people are not in the habit of creating estimates on a regular basis and being required to deliver results based on their estimates. Some people have a tendency to underestimate the workload because they are only looking at part of the task and may be missing some peripheral activities (such as producing documentation, completing testing, clarifying details, etc.). Some people have a tendency to overestimate the work involved to allow time to resolve a number of possible issues and ensure that delivery is still possible within the given timeframe.

In general, the inevitable uncertainty about exactly how long tasks within a project will take to be completed can make it very tempting to add a buffer to each individual work package. This can add up to create a huge total buffer for the project. Padding like this can increase the projected cost of the project to such an extent that a perfectly reasonable project is killed for lack of funding.

The section *Estimating Techniques* in *Part V Tools* on page 280 contains information on a number of different methods of estimating the time and resources required to complete a project or a work package. Use whichever method(s) are most appropriate for the task at hand.

> **Tipp:**
> The three point estimation method is estimation method that is particularly useful for resolving discussion about what a reasonable estimate is. *Three Point Estimation* is described on page 292.

Notes on Estimation:

It is important to okay the estimates of the work and resources with the person or team who will be responsible for completing the work package during the execution phase of the project. Failing to get agreement from the involved parties during the planning phase is almost guaranteed to cause problems during the execution phase.

An approach that often works well in practice is to get the team leads of the different skill areas that will be responsible for delivering each work package together in a room (or conference call) and have a planning session. The project manager (and/or the project sponsor) can explain the goals of the project in detail, and then the group can split the task into a set of work packages and assign people and costs to each of the work packages.

Confirm that the Required Resources Would Be Available to the Project

Before being able to approve the project, the project sponsor will need to know not only which resources are required to complete the project, but also whether or not the required resources would actually be available to the project should it move to the execution phase.

First of all, it is necessary to check if the necessary skills and resources are available within the organization. If not, then the project manager will need, with approval from

Project Management Practice

the project sponsor, to look outside the organization for the necessary skills and resources.

Even if the necessary skills and resources are available within the organization, they may not be available to the project. Generally speaking, organizations do not have skilled people sitting around with nothing to do. Similarly, organizations do not usually have expensive machinery sitting idle or leave large amounts of office space unused. So, the question is most likely to be one of prioritization: is this project more important to the organization than the purpose to which the required resources are currently allocated?

If there is an issue with prioritization of the necessary resources, then some kind of agreement will need to be reached. Ideally, both the PMO and the project sponsor will have received guidance from the executive management team regarding the relative priority of this project compared with other work that the organization is currently performing. This should be sufficient information to resolve any conflicts. If conflicts still exist, then a request needs to be made to the executive management team to set the correct prioritization for the project.

Often, the simplest method of confirming that the necessary resources can be made available to the project is to create the resource plan for the project. This is covered in more detail in the topic *The Resource Plan* on page 162.

If the required resources are not available, or cannot be made available, then the project has no chance of success and the project should not progress beyond this planning phase.

Notes on Resource Planning:

Do not forget to allow for planned absences such as vacation and training.

Ensure that the requested resources have been agreed to by the responsible line manager – especially if they are not directly involved in the planning discussions.

Getting a deputy named during the planning phase will help if the named person goes on vacation, becomes sick, or is otherwise suddenly unavailable. The deputy will be able to carry on the work and the project should not become delayed because a required expert is suddenly missing. While it should be possible to define a deputy for vacations, it may not always be possible to have a deputy available for unplanned absences. Many organizations simply do not have sufficient skilled people to define a deputy for every skill area in every project.

Whenever possible, get a specific person named as the deputy. This is better than a general agreement from the

Project Management Practice

line manager or team lead for that skill area that the work will be completed by an unspecified person because this allows the project manager to steer the named people directly.

CREATE THE PROJECT PLAN

When most people think of a project plan, they typically think of a Gantt chart. A Gantt chart is a simple diagram showing when each task starts and when each task finishes with any dependencies between the tasks added.

In fact, a Gantt Chart is more correctly one method of representing the delivery schedule, which is only a single component of the full project plan. The full project plan consists of the following components:

- The delivery schedule
- The resource plan
- The communications plan
- The risk mitigation plan (optional for projects which have only standard operational risks)

The resource plan and the delivery schedule are closely linked to one another. No delivery schedule will be reliable unless it has been confirmed that the resources required to complete the project will be available when they are needed. Therefore, it often makes sense to complete the resource plan and the delivery schedule together.

The communication plan is largely independent of the other plans. The purpose of the communication plan is to ensure that all project stakeholders are kept up to date on the status of the project.

The risk mitigation plan is also largely independent of the other plans and can be developed independently. The risk mitigation plan is intended to reduce the chance that unexpected events will:

- cause the project to fail
- require significant additional budget or time to be invested so that the work can be completed
- leave the project team unprepared

These components are described in more detail below.

The Delivery Schedule

The delivery schedule states when each work package will be started and when it will be completed. It also provides an overview of the dependencies between work packages and identifies which work packages can be completed in parallel.

It is normal that creating a delivery schedule is a repetitive process. First of all, each work package is planned using the time estimates supplied. Then, the schedule is checked for resource availability. Adjustments are made to the schedule to allow for resource availability, and the schedule is checked again.

For midsized, large, and long running projects, the resource plan is likely to change often during the

Project Management Practice

execution phase. In these cases, do not be too concerned about getting every work package perfectly planned in advance. Instead, make sure that sufficient resources will be made available so that the deliverables can be completed on time and leave it be. Creating a general resource plan, with detailed resource planning on a regular basis for the upcoming work packages, will be more practical.

It should be clear from the delivery schedule:

- Which work packages are being worked on at any one time
- By which date the individual work packages are expected to be delivered
- Any dependencies between work packages
- Which work could slip (be delayed) a little without delaying the final project delivery date and which work must be completed on time to maintain the final delivery date.

A Gantt Chart is an excellent tool for this purpose. Many software solutions are available which will generate a Gantt Chart for you and allow you to use it to track project progress during the execution phase. However, for straightforward projects with a small number of work packages or with very simple dependencies, then a simple spreadsheet works perfectly well.

Project Management Practice

Below is an example of a Gantt Chart which shows a delivery schedule which has not started yet. The expected start and end date of each work package can be easily identified on the chart. This example shows a more modern Gantt Chart which also includes the dependencies (network) between the work packages.

The critical path in this Gantt Chart is shown using dotted boxes to identify the work packages on the critical path. The work packages shown in full lines could be delayed slightly and the entire project could still be delivered on time. Obviously, if the work packages are delayed for too long, then this will also cause the entire project to be delayed. Critical paths are discussed in more detail in *Project Schedule, Network Diagram*, on page 300.

Sample Gantt Chart

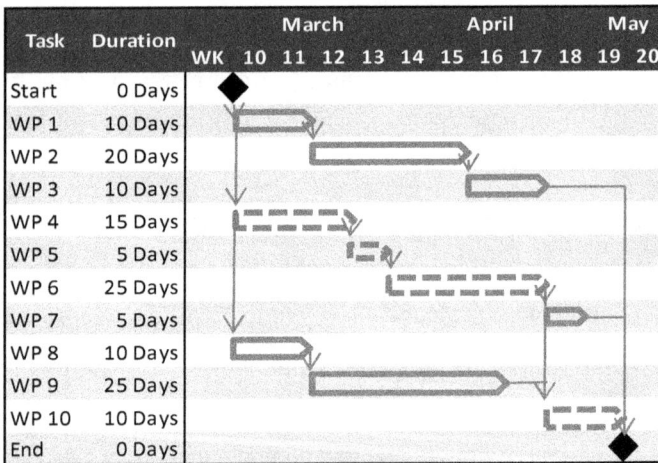

Task	Duration	WK	10	11	12	13	14	15	16	17	18	19	20
			March					April				May	
Start	0 Days												
WP 1	10 Days												
WP 2	20 Days												
WP 3	10 Days												
WP 4	15 Days												
WP 5	5 Days												
WP 6	25 Days												
WP 7	5 Days												
WP 8	10 Days												
WP 9	25 Days												
WP 10	10 Days												
End	0 Days												

Project Management Practice

Various alternatives to a Gantt Chart are available. For projects with relatively few interdependencies between work packages, an Action Item List (AIL), or a simple graph can be perfectly sufficient. For complex projects, Gantt Charts are recommended, with Network Diagrams being a possible alternative. Network diagrams and Gantt Charts are discussed in more detail in *Part V Tools, Project Schedule* on page 294.

Part V Tools, Project Schedule also discusses the different types of dependencies that are possible between work packages and gives examples of how the different types of dependency could be used.

The PMO should be able to provide information on how to access the organization's standard project scheduling tools or be able to make them available on request.

When the project schedule is being developed, keep in mind that it will be used to communicate progress to a number of stakeholders, each of whom may require a different level of detail. Management or the customer may find an overview that highlights the major blocks of completed and open work useful. The project manager and the project team are likely to need a far more detailed view to plan their activities on the individual work packages as effectively as possible.

Project Management Practice

It is important that the overall schedule is readily understood by the diverse people who will be using it. It may be sensible for the project manager to maintain a detailed schedule on a day-to-day basis for use by themselves and the project team. It may also be necessary to maintain a high-level project schedule for reporting purposes.

Notes on Project Schedule Development:

- Scheduling work packages to be completed in parallel:

  Do not forget while developing the project delivery schedule that even if two work packages are technically independent of each other and could be completed in parallel, resource constraints may force the work packages to be completed serially.

- The hours of work required to complete a task do not always equal the elapsed time until the task is completed:

  It is worthwhile to find out how much time people will have available to work on the project. Let us take an example of a single task that only requires eight hours of work. Theoretically, it could be completed in a single day. However, if in practice the expert assigned to the task has so many other tasks to perform that they can only spare an hour a day to spend on the project, then the task will take one and a half weeks to complete. Similar

Project Management Practice

considerations can apply to machinery and other specialized facilities.

- Compressing the time scale by adding more people:

A frequent approach to reducing the elapsed time required to complete a task is to add more people to the task. For example: If a single painter can paint a room in 4 hours then two painters should be able to paint the room in 2 hours.

In practice, however, every time that you add an extra person to a task, there is a need for them to coordinate their work with the other people already assigned to that task. (To use our simple example above, the two painters would need to agree to paint different walls to avoid each of them duplicating the other painter's work.) This means that there exists a small additional overhead to adding extra people to the task. If you add too many people, the coordination overhead can become so large that it is actually more effective to use less people.

It is worth being aware that some tasks simply cannot be completed faster by adding extra people. This is often the case when the production process requires a certain amount of time. (No matter how many painters that you add, you will still need to wait for the paint to dry…)

Project Management Practice

The Resource Plan

The goal of the resource plan is to describe which resources will be required and at which time they will be needed. Resources include the members of the project team, and any specialized equipment, machinery, or working areas.

Start with the deliverables and work packages that were created earlier in the planning process. From these it should be a relatively simple matter to extract information regarding which resources will be required. Putting this information together with the first draft of the delivery schedule will identify when the different resources will be required.

The next step is to check for resource availability:

- For how many hours a week / month will the required resources be available to the project?
- Are there particular time periods during the expected project duration when the resources will be unavailable due to other commitments?
  Other commitments could include planned absences, shift work, or higher priority work that is competing with this project.

The delivery schedule will most likely need to be adjusted to fit the availability of the required resources. After two or three iterations of reviewing both the resource plan and the project schedule, a schedule and resource plan should be available which most people can agree to – even if minor changes are still required to deal with unexpected events.

Notes on Resource Planning:

Individual work packages may slip forward or backwards by small amounts. Therefore, attempt to ensure that work packages are not planned to complete just before the planned absence of a subject matter expert. This helps to avoid the risk of a slight delay becoming a large one when the task can only be completed after the expert returns from their planned absence.

Team members can fall ill or otherwise be unexpectedly unavailable. Wherever possible, identify a deputy for each member of the project team. Add this information to the stakeholder list. Then, should a team member become unexpected unavailable, work on the project can continue.

The Communication Plan

On average, a project manager spends about 70% of their time involved in some form of communication. There will be regular meetings with the project with the project team to gather the status of the work completed so far. There will be regular meetings with the project sponsor to keep them informed of the overall project status. To facilitate

Project Management Practice

the meetings with the project sponsor, the project manager will need to provide reports showing the status of the project. These will include the progress made to date, any open issues, and the method by which the issues are expected to be resolved.

The different experts involved in producing the project results will need to inform each other of the status of their tasks. This is required to ensure that dependencies between different tasks are coordinated properly.

The project manager will need to manage communications with all the project stakeholders to keep them informed of the project progress and ensure that they are all still supportive of the project. This may mean that a general report on progress, perhaps in the form of newsletter, is required to keep all stakeholders aware of progress and any benefits achieved so far.

Unless all this communication is planned and organized, the project will feel very chaotic and it is highly likely that important information will not get to the right people at the right time.

A communication plan states how information will flow within the project.

- For meetings:
  - what the purpose of the meeting is

- o   how often will each meeting be held
- o   who is expected to attend each meeting
- o   how the results or actions of the meeting will be documented and distributed
- For reports:
  - o   what the purpose of the report is
  - o   how often the report will be created
  - o   who will the report be distributed to
  - o   who will create the report

Refer to *Communication Plan Template* on page 374 for an example of a communication plan template.

Create a Risk Mitigation Plan

A risk mitigation plan describes how the project team intends to reduce or avoid the risks to the project that are likely enough or significant enough to need attention.

The first step towards creating a risk mitigation plan is to identify the different risks associated with the project. Use input from the entire project planning team to ensure that as many risks as possible are identified and noted. A brainstorming session is an excellent forum to do this. No-one should be discouraged from identifying even seemingly silly risks during this initial risk identification step.

Project Management Practice

The next step is to quantify the risk to the organization. Two factors are important here:

1. How likely is it that the risk will become reality?
2. What is the impact to the project, and the organization, if the risk should become reality?

Risks with an extremely low probability of occurrence can generally be ignored unless the impact of the risk is exceptionally high. Risks that are more likely but will have negligible impact on the project can also be safely ignored. Also, standard operational risks should not require specific mitigation strategies from the project team. In case of doubt, the PMO or project sponsor should be able to provide guidance on what level of risk is considered acceptable within the organization and the risk management techniques that the project team should consider.

Having identified the risks that the project team needs to manage, the final step is to create a risk mitigation strategy. Risk mitigation strategies have the task of reducing or avoiding risk. The approach taken should be appropriate to the risk.

Refer to the section *Risk Management* in *Part V Tools*, on page 309 for more detailed information on how to manage risk.

Project Management Practice

It is important to spend time examining ways to effectively manage and reduce risk. It is equally important not to spend so much time looking at ways to avoid or minimize risk that the project fails to complete successfully. Keep the level of risk management appropriate to the size of the project.

Store all the Project Plans for Future Reference

Once the project plans have been created, store them in the central project repository provided by the PMO. These are the original plans on which the project sponsor will decide whether or not to execute the project. Assuming the project is approved, they will be required to manage the project during the execution phase.

Project Management Practice

COMPLETE THE BUSINESS CASE

One of the final tasks during the planning phase is to complete the business case for the project. The outline business case was created during the initiation phase and was made available to help guide the project planning team. Now, there should be sufficient information available to create a complete business case for the project. If there is insufficient information available to create a complete business case, then review the planning that has been completed so far and check that it is complete.

The project sponsor will be able to provide the project manager with guidelines on the level of detail required for the business case.

If the business case is not a compelling one, review this with the project sponsor. There may be a need to review the project goals and replan.

Notes on Completing the Business Case:

There are some projects that the organization is required to complete regardless of the results of the business case. Examples could be:

- It is necessary to obtain a certification required by the industry

Project Management Practice

- New legislation could have been introduced which the organization must conform to

In these kinds of situations, the business case reduces to: implement the project or stop doing business.

Other examples where a business case may be of little value include:

- The organization is entering a new field of strategic importance to the organization and the organization is aware that it will initially make a loss
- A new product being is being created which is so innovative that predicting sales is impossible

Under these circumstances, a formal business case is probably not helpful to the project sponsor or the executive management team and they may prefer not to one.

CREATE THE SCOPE STATEMENT

The scope statement is one of the most important project documents. The scope statement summarizes all the information gathered during the planning phase of the project in one place. It states what the project will deliver, when it will be delivered, and what resources are required to deliver the project successfully.

The project sponsor will probably make their decision on whether to invest in the project based on the contents of the scope statement.

Even though the full details of the project plan cannot be directly included in the project scope statement, ensure that the most important information is available:

- What will the project deliver? (What are the benefits to the organization of completing the project?)
- What will the project not deliver? (Is the project scope clear?)
- Which resources are required to complete the project? (How much will it cost)?
- Would the necessary resources be available? (Is it possible for the organization to complete the project successfully?)

Project Management Practice

- How long will it take the project to complete? (How long will it take until the organization receives the benefits of performing the project?)
- Are their particular risks inherent in the project, which are not normal operational risks and that should be highlighted to the project sponsor?

By agreeing to start the project, the project sponsor commits, on behalf of the organization, to make the resources described in the scope statement available to the project manager. In return, the project sponsor expects to receive the project deliverables according to the time line described in the project scope statement.

Refer to *Scope Statement Template* on page 375 for an example of a scope statement template.

Notes on Creating the Scope Statement:

Since the project sponsor will most likely base their "go" / "no go" decision for the project on the scope statement, it is important that all the information relevant to making the decision to continue with the project is summarized in the scope statement in an easily digestible form. If the scope statement is difficult to understand or read, then it adds another barrier to moving the project to the execution phase. If acceptable within your organization, consider changing the format from a printed document to a presentation slide pack.

Project Management Practice

Ensure that any planning assumptions are highlighted in the scope statement. The project sponsor then has the chance to confirm that the assumptions made were reasonable ones.

FORMALLY COMMIT TO THE PROJECT

At this point, the organization knows as much about the project as it is possible to know without actually starting the project.

- The project goals are clear
- The deliverables which the organization intends to produce in order to meet the project goals are known
- It is confirmed that the project deliverables (internal project view) will together to meet the project goals (external project view)
- The necessary resources (budget, machinery, project team, etc.) to complete the project successfully and the availability of those resources, are known
- A business case for the project is available
- The time schedule for the project is known

The project manager now needs to present this information to the project sponsor so that the project sponsor can make a decision to commit the organization to the project or not. This will normally be completed in a review meeting of the project scope statement between the project sponsor and the project manager.

The project sponsor will discuss any necessary changes to the project scope with the project manager. The project

Project Management Practice

sponsor will then give a formal approval (or not) for the project to move to the execution phase.

Once the scope statement has been agreed to, store it in the central project repository provided by the PMO along with the project approval documentation (typically an email) from the project sponsor. Because of the importance of agreeing to a scope statement, some organizations require a personal signature from the project sponsor and the project manager to show that the scope statement has been agreed to.

In the future, changes to the project scope statement will need to be approved by both the project sponsor and the project manager. This is necessary to protect the project from "scope slip".

Scope Slip:

Scope slip is the term used when the project manager or members of the project team are asked to perform extra work as part of the project. Scope slip has been the downfall of a number of projects.

It frequently starts off as a single, small, innocuous request to perform a task closely related to the project goals or deliverables. If the request really is of negligible effort and supports the project either directly or indirectly, then there is unlikely to be a problem with the project team

---

taking on the extra work. In some cases, though, the requests made to the project team can grow to be significant pieces of work, or the number of minor requests can increase to the point that the project team is required to commit a lot of extra effort to deal with them. This impacts the project team's ability to deliver the project results. Completing the extra work means that there are insufficient resources available to complete the original project goals. The project then goes over budget, in delay, or fails to complete the deliverables at all.

For this reason, the project team needs to be aware of the possible impact of scope slip and ensure that any request made to them is approved by the project manager. If the project manager has even the slightest concern that the extra work could impact the project's ability to deliver the project results, then the request to complete extra work should be presented to the project sponsor with an estimate of the additional resources required to complete the extra work. If the project sponsor agrees to fund the additional resources and is willing to accept the related delays in final project completion, then the additional work can be added to the scope of the project.

Consider recommending that the requested additional work be implemented in a subsequent project instead of increasing the scope of the existing project. In many industries and organizations, this is a constructive

Project Management Practice

alternative to expanding the scope of an existing project.

CHAPTER 16.

PROJECT EXECUTION & MONITORING

A typical project spends more time in the execution phase than in any other phase. It is also the area that is least supported by prevailing project management theory. This is because the actual work performed during project execution is different for each project. Even though the actual work that will be completed will be different for every project, the project management process still remains consistent.

From a process viewpoint, the basic steps to be taken in this phase are:

1. Complete any administrative tasks
2. Hold Kick-off Meeting
3. Distribute work packages
4. Execute work packages
5. Monitoring
6. Plan changes
7. Report progress
8. Implement change requests
9. Respond to issues
10. Respond to scope change requests

Project Management Practice

Steps 1 & 2 happen once at the beginning of the project execution and monitoring phase.

Steps 3 to 8 repeat continuously throughout the project execution phase until all the work packages have been successfully completed.

Steps 9 & 10 will be performed if and when they become necessary.

During the planning phase of the project, the project manager only had responsibility for the small number of team members who were required to complete the planning. It is also unlikely that many issues occurred during the planning phase. This picture changes significantly once the project moves into the execution and monitoring phase.

This phase is where the capabilities of the project manager will be tested. Of course, the project manager will need to ensure that the cycle of steps from "distribute work packages" to "implement internal changes" is working smoothly. However, they are also likely to be spending a significant portion of their time dealing with issues related to the project or the project team.

Project Management Practice

COMPLETE ANY ADMINISTRATIVE TASKS

Completing administrative tasks is just a preparation step before the whole execution and monitoring phase starts.

Before holding the kick-off meeting and formally starting the project in the eyes of the project team, it is a good idea to ensure that all the administrative tasks related to the project have been completed.

- Confirm that the booking code for the project is available and usable
- Confirm that the planning information is in a form which can be readily understood by the team who will use it
- Confirm that the PMO is aware that the project has completed planning and is now entering the execution phase

Project Management Practice

HOLD THE PROJECT KICK-OFF MEETING

The project manager will need to organize a kick-off meeting including all the team members. The project manager and the project sponsor have probably spent quite some time working on this project already. However, it is important to remember that this is the first introduction to the project for many members of the project team,.

The main goals of the kick-off meeting are:

- To ensure that everyone involved in the project team is aware of the overall project goals.
  (It is recommended to state the goals, not only in terms of what results the project will deliver, but also in terms of what benefits the organization expects to receive from the project.)
- To ensure that everyone involved in the project knows all the team members and what their respective roles are
- To ensure that everyone involved in the project knows what their tasks are and how these fit together to achieve the desired project results
- To explain how communication within the project will happen
- To explain the budget for the project and the cost control measures which will be in place

Project Management Practice

(reporting of hours spent, machine usage time, cash out, ...)

- To motivate the project team to commit to delivering the project results.

   (Ideally, the team will feel that they "own" the project and are personally responsible for their part and responsible as a group for delivering the final results.)

- To officially start the project in the eyes of the project team

The ideal situation is to have everyone in the same room for the kick-off meeting. However, if the project team members are spread over several different locations, getting everyone in the same room may be too costly or impractical. In this case, alternatives, such as a telephone conference, would need to be found.

The most important task during the meeting is to make sure everyone understands what they need to do and how their work fits together with everyone else's work to complete the final project results. However, do not underestimate the importance of motivating the project team. Many of the team will have other demands on their time and / or will be working in relative isolation on their part of the project results. In order for the project to be a success, they need to be motivated to get their part done on time.

Project Management Practice

It is often worth reminding everyone on the team that, if they are asked to complete extra work that is not included in the current scope or work packages, then this request will need to be cleared by the project manager. The project manager will in turn clear it with the project sponsor if necessary.

DISTRIBUTE WORK PACKAGES

Distributing the work packages is the start of the main process cycle that occurs during the execution and monitoring phase of the project.

Directly after the kick-off meeting, the project manager will need to distribute the work packages that can be started immediately to the project team members who will be responsible for completing them. Check that the project team member understands the task at hand. If the task will not be finished by the next regular project team meeting, then make sure that the team member knows they will be expected to provide a progress statement at the next team meeting.

As individual work packages are completed, the prerequisites for other work packages will be met. The project manager will need to check which additional work packages can be released and distributed to the project team. These newly released work packages will in turn need to be tracked by the project manager. This cycle continues until all the work packages for the project are completed.

Project Management Practice

EXECUTE THE WORK PACKAGES

Distributing the work packages to the project team is relatively simple. Actually getting the work done on time is more of a challenge. Typically, project team members are not assigned solely to one particular project, but have other work to do as well. The other work can come from their line manager or from other projects.

Project managers do not normally have disciplinary authority over their team members, so they must find other methods of making sure that the work is completed on time. Here are some helpful techniques for getting the task completed on time and up to quality standards:

- Keep up regular contact with the team
- Ensure that the importance of the project to the organization has been clearly communicated to each team member
- Ensure that the line managers of the project team members understand the importance of the project to the organization and are supporting the project
- Deal with reported delays in a consistent and constructive manner. If a project manager just shrugs their shoulders and accepts a delay, then the message is sent that the project or task is not important. If the project manager follows up with the team member to identify the cause of the

Project Management Practice

delay and ensures any issues are resolved, then the message is sent that the project work is important and requires the attention of the project team

MONITORING

Monitoring is the project manager's most important task once the project is in the execution phase. If this is not done well, issues cannot be caught and resolved early and the project is likely to be delivered late and/or over budget.

The task here is not just to confirm that the planned work is being completed on time, it is also necessary to check the other factors that will affect the project team's ability to deliver the desired results. As a minimum, the project manager will need to monitor the following:

- Progress: Are the work packages completing on time?
- Costs: Is there sufficient budget remaining to complete the uncompleted work?
- Quality: Are the quality expectations set at the beginning of the project being met?
- Risk:
  - Can any known risks be eliminated from the risk register because the work has been completed and the risk is no longer valid?
  - Has any improved method of mitigating a known risk become apparent?
  - Have any new risks become apparent which need to be tracked or managed?

Project Management Practice

186

As per the communication plan, the project manager will hold regular project team meetings. These are used to gather the current status from each team member and to allow each team member to inform the rest of the team of any issues that they need to be aware of. In particular, the project team will need to be informed of any issues that will affect the delivery schedule, as this may affect when their tasks need to be performed.

Keep the time spent on discussing issues in the team meeting to a reasonable level to avoid wasting the team's time. In particular, avoid using the team meeting to find a solution to an issue. Organize separate meetings to resolve issues, with just the relevant team members attending. There are several good reasons for this:

- The members of the team who are not needed to resolve the issue can use their time constructively on other tasks
- It also helps to keep the team meeting focused on status and information exchanges
- It discourages team members from waiting for the team meeting before raising an issue with the project manager

Obviously, just gathering the status of the project is not enough. The project manager has full responsibility for successful delivery of the project, not just full responsibility for reporting any issues! So, implicit in the

Project Management Practice

monitoring task is the task to take action if something is going wrong with the project.

Monitoring Progress

Progress monitoring has the task of checking that the work packages being completed according to the project schedule. If this is not the case, then the cause needs to be investigated and resolved.

Often, regular progress checks with the project team will be sufficient to keep the project on track. However, in some cases, just motivating people to get their tasks done on time will not be enough. There are several options that a project manager may consider to bring a project back onto schedule. These include:

Change the Delivery Schedule

The simplest solution, and often the best, is to request a change to extend the project delivery schedule. The project will still finish within the budget, meet quality standards, and will have no significant additional risk. If the delay is acceptable to the project sponsor and the end customer, then this is the simplest solution and generally the best option.

However, before going to the project sponsor with a change request to extend the project delivery time, consider the other options listed here and present the

Project Management Practice

project sponsor with some alternatives. This makes it clear that the project manager has done their job and examined all possibilities before making a recommendation. Any project manager who only recommends a project delay to deal with every issue will quickly be seen as ineffective.

Fast Tracking

Fast tracking involves executing two tasks in parallel (or overlapping), which were originally planned to be executed sequentially.

Let me return to the example of a house being built to help explain this idea. There are currently two tasks that need to be completed:

- The electricians need to wire the house
- The plasterers need to plaster all the walls in the house after the electricians have finished

In the original plan, the electricians were due to complete their work and then the plasterers were due to come in afterwards. However, a delay elsewhere means the project manager is looking for ways to speed up delivery of the whole project.

Fast tracking the tasks would mean that the two teams work in the house at the same time. As soon as the electricians finish a room, the plasterers would move into the room and plaster it. Because the two tasks are now overlapping, the time taken to finish both tasks has been reduced.

Obviously, this method of completing tasks in parallel often increases costs if something goes wrong. In the example above, if the electricians had discovered a mistake in the wiring as part of their final checks, then correcting that mistake is more difficult and costly now that the room has been plastered than it would have been under the original plan.

Fast tracking requires increased communication and adds risk to the project. In the right circumstances, however, it can be very effective and involve little or no added cost to the project.

Crashing

Crashing a project does not mean to "drive it into a wall". Crashing is a trade-off between speed and money and includes any method of decreasing the time taken to deliver the project results that requires an increase to the overall project cost.

For example, the project manager may consider that a reduction in time would be achieved by investing in improved tools for the project team. Alternatively, increasing the size of the project team in a particular skill area might be a method of speeding up delivery of the project results.

Note that adding extra people to a task is not always a good solution. When considering adding people to a project already in execution, always consider:

- How long will it take the new team member to learn enough to become productive?
- How much time will the rest of the team need to invest in supporting new team members?
- What is the impact that the increased amount of communication and co-ordination will have on the effectiveness of the team's overall performance?
- Is the task suitable for having multiple people working on it? Some tasks are simply not two-people jobs.

Changing the Scope

In some projects, there are relatively unimportant tasks that require considerable time and effort to complete. In these circumstances, it is worth considering requesting that these low value deliverables be removed from the scope of the project. This may save the time required to ensure that the main project deliverables are available on time. As always, any change in scope will require an

Project Management Practice

approval from the project sponsor and the project manager.

Changing the Quality

It may be possible to reduce the quality standard for some work packages without significantly reducing the overall quality of the project results. Any change in quality, in any phase of the project, will require the approval of the project sponsor.

Cost Management

The overall goal of cost management is to ensure that the remaining project budget is sufficient to complete the remaining project tasks.

If a cost code is being used to track project expenditure, then it is relatively simple to identify the costs that the project has produced to date. Deduct this sum from the original project budget, and the remaining project budget is clear. This very simple form of accounting is typical for a project. Complex accounting techniques are normally not required.

There are not usually many options available to reduce costs in the final stages of project delivery. Therefore, it is important to ensure that work packages do not start to overrun on costs at any time during execution.

Project Management Practice

If a project does start to overrun the budget, then it is important to make the project sponsor aware of this as early as possible during project execution. The earlier that budget overrun is identified, the more chance there is of reducing the total over-expenditure of the project. The project sponsor will need to be aware of the alternatives and what the impact to the project would be if one of the alternatives would be implemented. Techniques for dealing with a budget overrun include:

Delaying Delivery to Reduce Costs

Quite often, a project will make an investment to reduce the time taken to deliver the project to a tight timeline. The investment could be in extra resources, renting better tools, hiring expensive experts, or some other cost.

If this investment is not already a sunk cost, then by not making that investment any more, it may be possible to trade an increase in delivery time for a reduced cost.

This is effectively the opposite of *Crashing*, which was described on page 190.

Changing the Scope

There may be some work packages or deliverables included in the scope which add very little additional value to the whole project. Removing these low value deliverables from the scope of the project may save the money required to ensure that the main project goals can be delivered.

Changing the Quality

It may be possible to reduce the quality standard for some work packages without significantly reducing the overall quality of the project results. Any change in quality, in any phase of the project, will require the approval of the project sponsor.

Increasing the Available Budget

There may be good reasons why the original budget was underestimated. In this case, it is worth explaining the reasons to the project sponsor and see if a budget increase can be organized. Definitely have other options prepared.

Quality Management

The goal of quality management within a project is to ensure that the project results are meeting the quality standards defined in the initiation or planning phase of the project.

To make sure that the project results meet the quality standards set, the project manager will need to focus on two topics: the processes used to create the results, and the fitness of results for the purpose intended.

Project Management Practice

Changing the overall quality of the results produced has an effect on every part of the project. It will definitely affect the budget, the time taken to produce the results and, most likely, the scope of the project as well.

Risk Management

The main task of risk management is to help the project team avoid issues whenever possible. Issues that would seriously impact the ability of the project team to complete their work, or issues that would damage the organization as a whole, need to be avoided.

The initial register of significant risks was created during the planning phase of the project. As the project progresses, the risks will change. The risk register will need to be updated to reflect this.

If the organization is managing risk centrally, then the PMO will need to be informed that the risk register has been updated.

The main task of regular risk management during execution is to review the risk register. It is particularly important to do this regularly for long running or riskier projects. Reviewing the risk register includes:

- Removing any risks which are no longer valid

Project Management Practice

195

- Checking if an improved risk mitigation strategy is available
- Adding any newly identified risks

Risk management is covered in greater detail in *Chapter 23, Risk Management*, which starts on page 309.

Remove any Risks Which Are No Longer Valid

This is the most common form of update to the risk register during execution. As work packages complete, it will no longer be possible for some risks to occur. For example, the risk of non-delivery of an important component no longer exists once that component has been delivered by the chosen supplier.

Any risk that can no longer become an issue needs to be removed from the risk register.

Improved Risk Mitigation Strategy

During project execution, the project team may identify an improved risk mitigation strategy that was not apparent during planning. If this is the case, and the project manager supports the change, then the old risk mitigation strategy can be replaced with the new one.

The risk register needs to be updated to show the improvement.

Add Newly Identified Risks

As the project progresses, risks may become apparent which were not seen during the planning process. If these risks meet the project's criteria to be managed regularly, then these risks will need to be added to the risk register together with the chosen risk mitigation strategy.

Project Management Practice

PLAN CHANGES

A need to make a change to the project can come from s number of sources. Examples include:

- One of the monitoring tasks has identified an issues which requires a change to the project to be resolved
- A scope change has been requested and approved
- The project team may have identified an opportunity which requires a change before it can be take advantage of

A change can have a major impact on the project and require significant replanning. However, a change can also be almost insignificant and easily achieved by the project team with very little effort.

The following diagram provides an overview of the different types of change and the planning effort required:

Project Management Practice

Project Change Types Grouped by Impact and Source

		Impact	
		Minor	**Major**
Source	**Issue**	• No formal change required • Project manager agrees to changes with the project team, and then implement them	• Formal change required • Project manager agrees to the change with the project team and then gets the project sponsor to agree to the change request
	Change request	• Insignificant impact to the project team's work • Formal change required, but agreement can normally be reached easily	• Major impact to the project team's work • Formal change required • The project will need to be re-planned in whole or in part to accommodate this change request

Project Management Practice

	Impact	
	Minor	**Major**
Enhancements	• Little replanning is required to take advantage of this improvement • No formal change required • Project manager agrees to changes with the project team and implements them	• Significant replanning is required to take advantage of this improvement • Formal change required • Project manager agrees to the change with the project team and then gets the project sponsor to agree to the change request

A project change means changing how the project is planned and executed. Planning a change means: identifying what needs to be changed, identifying what impact the change will have on the whole project, and getting the agreement necessary to implement the change.

Almost without exception, a change will affect at least one component of the project plan (project schedule, resource

Project Management Practice

plan, communication plan, or risk mitigation plan). Where a formal change is required, the relevant documents will need to be changed and presented to the project sponsor.

The following sections look at each of the different project change types listed above.

Change Planning in Response to Minor Issues

Minor issues are issues that the project manager can solve, without any real impact to the project plan.

Typical examples of minor issues are:

- The project team can solve the issue themselves and the work package can still be delivered on time
- A work package is delayed. Some communication may be necessary to reschedule the dependent tasks, but the overall project schedule is not impacted in any significant way. In particular, the delivery of the project results will not be delayed
- A member of the team is leaving, but a replacement has been found and sufficient time is available for a handover of the open tasks

A formal project change should not be necessary even if a minor update to the project schedule, resource plan, or other plans is required.

Dealing with minor issues quickly and effectively is often a key factor in ensuring the minor issued does not become a major issue later on.

The section Respond to Issues on page 215 provides advice on how to deal with the most common issues that a project manager is likely to face.

Change Planning in Response to Major Issues

Major issues are issues that require significant replanning of the project.

Typical examples of major issues are:

- The project results will be significantly delayed
- Additional resources need to be allocated to the project for it to complete on time and within quality
- The project results will not meet the overall goals and requirements of the project without making significant changes to the project deliverables

The project sponsor will need to be involved. They will need to understand:

- Why the change is necessary
- What the impact of the change will be

Project Management Practice

- What the impact of not performing the change will be

Refer also to *Requests for Decisions* on page 227 for more details on obtaining a decision from the project sponsor.

Change Planning in Response to Minor Scope Changes

Almost all projects require minor details to be clarified. To take our example of building the house, at some point the family will wish to select the tiles for the bathroom or the carpets for the floor. These are minor details. The team knows that the jobs need to be done and that the customer is unlikely to have made a final decision before the work is commissioned. These tasks have an impact on the overall cost of the project and will need to be formally agreed to. For example, the tiles finally chosen by the family for the bathroom may cost significantly more than the amount originally budgeted.

These kinds of minor details can normally be covered by getting the request in writing and agreeing to an additional payment to cover the costs that were not in the original budget.

Sometimes, as the project progresses, it may become clear that minor changes to the project scope are necessary which were not apparent during the initial planning phase. An example of a minor scope change would be a change of

Project Management Practice

a deliverable, which has not yet been started by the project team, and requires no significant changes to the resource planning.

These kinds of change request are normally considered to be perfectly reasonable and can generally be implemented without any major effort by the project team.

Caution:

If there are large numbers of minor scope changes, then the project manager will need to keep an eye on the additional costs and delays being created by repeatedly replanning small parts of the project. Eventually, the total effort of responding to many small changes will affect the project team's ability to deliver the results on time and within budget.

If the change in scope means that the project scope statement is no longer correct, then the scope statement will need to be updated. The updated scope statement will need to be agreed to by the project sponsor and the project manager. Even for or a minor scope change this is necessary. It ensures that there are no resultant discussions during project closure about the project having failed to deliver on the agreed project scope.

Project Management Practice

Change Planning in Response to Major Scope Changes

Major scope change can be forced onto the project team from the outside. Examples are:

- a major deliverable is no longer required by the receiver of the project results
- The customer requires that the project goal be expanded to include an additional major deliverable
- The funding for the project has been cut significantly

These things happen and are extremely frustrating when they do. No one enjoys seeing several thousand hours of work being wasted, or getting close to the end of a project only to have another major deliverable added.

The first step is to look why the major scope change is being requested. Often this will point to some failure in the project management process that should be fixed before the organization attempts a similar project in the future.

If the project has had the funding cut, follow the advice under *Closing Failed or Incomplete Projects* on page 250.

If the project team is being asked to deliver to an expanded scope, then this could be due to positive recognition of the good work being completed. The new

Project Management Practice

deliverable will need to be planned and then delivered. It is well worth considering putting the new deliverable into a follow-up project. In some cases, the project sponsor may prefer expand the project scope in order to avoid the administrative overhead of creating a new project.

From a planning perspective, the steps are clear:

- The details of the scope change will need to be analyzed and fully understood
- The impact on the project will need to be assessed
- The project will need to be re-planned in whole or in part to reflect the change in scope
- The project sponsor and the project manager will need to agree to the updated project scope

Change Planning in Response to Enhancements

While working on the project, a member of the project team may recognize that performance could be improved by changing the way the work is being completed. They would then present their idea to the project manager.

First of all, the project manager needs to examine the project as a whole to ensure that there is an overall benefit. It can happen that one specialist has an idea for reducing their own workload, but introducing this change would create far more work for other team members and the project team would suffer as a whole. In other

Project Management Practice

instances, the idea presented could produce significant improvements in the team's ability to deliver the project results.

When an idea for an enhancement is implemented, the person who had the idea should be publicly recognized. This helps to encourage the project team to presented further ideas. If the idea presented will not be used, take the time to explain one-on-one why the idea could not be implemented. It is important that the creative people in the team who are coming up with ideas for improvements feel that their ideas are being taken seriously. Remember that it is better to have someone on the team who generates five ideas of which only two can be implemented, than having someone on the team who does not generates any ideas at all.

If the enhancement can be implemented without any major changes to the project plan or project scope, then the project manager can implement the improvement directly. If implementing the enhancement will cause a major restructuring of the project or significant replanning, then the approval of the project sponsor will be required before the change can be implemented.

Project Management Practice

REPORT PROGRESS

Reporting is necessary to provide regular status updates to the project sponsor and other significant stakeholders. They will all want to be regularly reassured that the project is progressing smoothly. The communication plan lists which reports need to be created and how often they will be distributed.

The project manager will need to ensure that all the information that is required for the various reports is gathered on time. The goal is to ensure that there is time to prepare the report thoroughly, but it is still up to date. If this is not possible under the current communication plan, then it should be reviewed and any necessary changes made.

The Steering Board Report

The steering board report is probably the most important report that the project manager will need to produce on a regular basis. This report informs the project sponsor of the progress which the project team is making.

The general rule here is to produce a simple report (to ensure that progress is clearly documented), and then hold a short meeting to discuss the status as shown by the report.

Project Management Practice

The steering board report should show the status of the project overall, the status of the work packages currently in progress, the latest work packages which have completed, the work packages due to start next, any major risks or issues, and any decision that needs the input of the project sponsor.

- The status of the project overall:
    - If using a traffic light code, then use a clear guideline. For example:
    - Green: Everything is going according to plan.
    - Yellow: The project has some issues, but the project team expects to be able to resolve them with the resources that have been made available to them
    - Red: The project has issues that can only be resolved with assistance from outside the project team
    - If using a Gantt chart, include a line showing the current date as well as the progress towards each mile stone
- The status of the work packages currently in progress:
    - List all work packages which have been started but have not yet completed
    - If the work packages will take some time to complete, give the expected

completion date and some indication of the progress made

- The latest work packages which have been completed:
  - List all the work packages that have been delivered since the last report
  - If each work package takes a considerable time to complete, then show the last 3-4 work packages which were completed along with their completion dates
- The work packages due to start next:
  - In particular, list any work packages that are expected to start before the next project report is due
  - If each work package takes considerable time to complete, then show the next 3-4 work packages which are due to start with their expected start dates
- Any risks or issues which need to come to the attention of the project sponsor
- Any decisions which need to be made but which are beyond the authority of the project manager
- Refer to *Requests for Decisions* on page 227 for advice on preparing a decision request

All this information can be shown on two or three presentation slides or one to two pages of a report. Keep the main body of the report short and to the point. Add

Project Management Practice

extra slides / pages if you need to present a particular issue in depth. Putting each decision request on a separate slide / page improves focus and clarity during discussion.

The following slides show a sample project steering report template that can be used to present the main information listed above. The full *Steering Board Report Template* can be found on page 377. A similar format could also be used for a paper-based report.

Sample Report Template

Project Description		Project Milestones / Activities	Due Date
<Short project description>		<Milestone 1>	YYYY-MM-TT
		<Milestone 2>	
		<Milestone 3>	

<Project Name>
PM: <Project Manager>   Project Scope Summary

Project Goals
<Goal 1>
<Goal 2>
<Goal 3>

Project Management Practice

<Project Name> PM: <Project Manager>			Project Status: ⊙○○ Support from SB requested: No Scope Change request: No	

Current Milestones / Activities	Date	Status	Date	Achieved Results
Bla bla black sheep	YY-MM-DD	⊙○○	YY-MM-DD	Bla bla black sheep : Part 3

Risks & Issues	Measures taken	Due Date
Bla bla white sheep	Dye wool black	YYYY-MM-TT

Newsletters

It may be necessary to send out general information on the progress of the project to a wider audience. This information is usually sent in the form of a newsletter. This kind of general information is typically produced far less often than the steering board report.

The main purpose of a newsletter is to maintain the support of a wide base of stakeholders for the project.

When preparing a newsletter, it is normal to highlight the successes that the project has achieved. It is also worth noting that most of the audience will only skim the newsletter. So give each topic a clear headline so that the reader can quickly identify the topics that interest them.

Project Management Practice

As a general rule, a newsletter should not include more than six topics.

Other Reports

Most projects will require additional reports that are specific to that particular project. Review the communications plan regularly to ensure that all reports or other communications are made to ensure that all the stakeholders in the project are kept informed. Ideally, regular communication with the project stakeholders should not just report the status but also be aimed at keeping their support as the project progresses.

Normally, the project manager is responsible for producing reports. Even if they have assistance in producing the reports, the project manager will still need to review, agree to, and potentially present the reports. It is important to keep this reporting workload to a minimum so that it is possible to focus on getting the project work done. Therefore, it is worth making an effort to reduce the number of reports being produced to a minimum. Engage the support of the PMO if necessary to align reporting requirements within the organization. Where reports cannot be reused directly, attempt to reuse the same information in the various reports. Aside from reducing the reporting workload, this also ensures that a consistent message is sent to all stakeholders.

Project Management Practice

IMPLEMENT CHANGE REQUESTS

Implementing changes is the final step in the main execution and monitoring cycle.

The changes, which were planned earlier in the cycle, will have been agreed to during the presentation of the steering board report. Now that agreement has been reached, the planned changes will need to be implemented.

Any updated project plans will need to be stored in the central documentation repository. The changes will need to be explained to the project team so that they can make any adjustments necessary to their work.

RESPOND TO ISSUES

If the organization has successfully completed many projects similar to the one currently being attempted, then it is reasonable to expect the project to run smoothly. If, however, the project is doing something quite innovative, then issues are to be expected.

Most projects will have some minor issues, which the project manager will need to respond to and resolve. Some projects will suffer from one or more major issues that will require the attention of the project manager and other stakeholders. These issues will need to be managed properly (de-escalation), to ensure that once solved, they do not occur again.

The most frequent issues and some suggestions on how to approach them are listed in the table below.

Project Management Practice

The Most Frequently Occurring Project Issues

Issue	Suggestions
Key project members are suddenly unavailable due to illness or other unplanned personal absence.	Projects rarely have the kind of backup available that would be considered a must in an operational environment. If the missing project member is going to have a significant impact on the project team's ability to deliver the results, then ensure that the project sponsor is informed directly. If the person is expected to be unavailable for a significant length of time, negotiate with the line manager of the relevant skill area for a replacement. If the line manager is not able to provide a suitable alternative, involve the project sponsor to discuss sourcing the skill externally or to review the in-house priorities within the relevant skill area.

Issue	Suggestions
Key project members or other resources are not available due to higher priority work in the organization	This situation needs to be raised with the project sponsor. If the competing workload is really the higher priority, then either an alternative way forward needs to be found (external support, search for an alternative but comparable solution) or the project sponsor may decide that the organization will accept the delay in delivery. If the delay is accepted, then the decision needs to be documented and the project schedule and resource plan reworked to create a plan that the project team can deliver. The updated project plan will need to be approved by the project sponsor.

Project Management Practice

Issue	Suggestions
The work estimate was too low and there is insufficient budget or time to complete the remaining work	This issue needs to be discussed with the project sponsor as soon as it is identified. If the incorrect work estimate is identified early, the project manager and the project sponsor have the chance to renegotiate for additional budget and resources, assuming that the need can be clearly justified. If the project will not receive the required additional budget and resources, then the project team will probably fail to deliver the expected results. The project sponsor then has the opportunity to stop the project early and reduce any related financial losses.

Issue	Suggestions
As work on the project has progressed, it has become obvious that a task needs to be added to fulfil the major project requirements, even though this is not listed in the project deliverables	The issue here is that, during the execution phase of the project, it has become apparent that the internal view of the project (the deliverables) does not match the external view of the project (the project goals). Similarly to the work estimate being too low, this issue needs to be raised with the project sponsor as soon as it is identified. Again, if additional budget and resources are not made available to the project then the project will fail. It is easier to negotiate this early on in the project rather than just before expected delivery of the completed project results.

Project Management Practice

Issue	Suggestions
Scope slip: The project team or the project manager have been asked to add a number of seemingly minor tasks to the scope of the project, but the timeline, budget, and available resources have remained the same. Now the project is likely to be delivered late, over budget, or both.	Scope slip can be an insidious disease that has caused the failure of many a project. In essence, scope slip is caused by someone taking advantage of the good will of the project manager or project team to get additional work done which may be related to the project deliverables, but is not included in the current project scope. To help avoid this, implement a robust change management process and ensure that all the project team are aware that any scope changes need to be approved by the project sponsor. Once scope slip has occurred, it is more difficult to deal with. Explain to the project sponsor the extra work that was performed. Negotiate to get the scope expanded to include this work and have the budget increased accordingly.

Project Management Practice

Issue	Suggestions
The project team is being regularly interrupted by different people to ask about the project status.	This costs valuable time and eats steadily away at valuable resources. The cause of the issue is typically poor communication of the project status to all the relevant stakeholders. Ask the requestors to send their request for updates and information directly to the project manager. The project manager should review and update the communications plan to keep all the stakeholders informed of the project status. Ensure that stakeholders are aware that they will be getting regular status updates and that meetings are available to discuss any questions, concerns, or issues that people may have regarding the project.

Project Management Practice

De-escalation Management

De-escalation management has the goal of taking an escalated situation, resolving it, and making sure that it stays resolved – permanently.

The concept originated in the operations arena but it can be usefully applied in project management as well. The underlying assumption is that every issue or customer complaint costs time, effort, and money to resolve and that it is cheaper to resolve the issue once and for all, rather than deal with the same issue repeatedly.

Major issues requiring high management attention and detailed communication of the resolution process, take large amounts of time and effort to resolve. Keeping issues and escalations to a minimum, helps to optimize resource usage and keep operational costs low.

The principles behind de-escalation management are that once an issue has been escalated via the organization's escalation process, then that issue is not considered to be resolved until:

- The original issue is resolved
- The root cause of the issue is identified and understood

- Steps have been taken to ensure that the root cause of the issue is resolved so that the original issue will not reoccur

This seems a lot of effort at first. It is very tempting to just solve the immediate issue and move on. But, in practice, it really does save time to get the underlying issues solved.

Pre-emptive De-escalation Management:

A major escalation almost always involves significant extra effort by the project team. There is the overhead of frequent additional reporting, additional work to resolve the situation, and extra tasks which were not planned into the project budget which now need to be performed.

In some cases, a major escalation involving a significant team effort is justified. For instance, a serious risk has become an issue, or during the project it has become obvious that the assumptions for the project contained a serious error.

More often, though, how the issues is dealt with initially makes the difference between keeping an issue a minor issue and resolving it quietly within the normal project process, and having a major escalation with management and possibly customer involvement.

Project Management Practice

223

Ideally, any response to being informed about an issue will show that the issue:

- has been understood
- is being taken seriously by the person / project team dealing with it

The response also informs the person with the issue when they can expect either the next update or a resolution.

> One of the first project managers that I trained came from an operations background where response time was a key performance indicator. Early on in his first project he was notified by the customer of an issue. He responded quickly to the customer email with:
>
> ".. I have checked and can confirm that [the issue] exists. Best regards, ..."
>
> The trainee PM felt that they had done a good job by responding quickly to the customer's issue.
>
> As you might imagine, the issue landed on my desk within a couple of hours as the customer escalated the issue. The customer (quite understandably) did not feel that the issue was being taken seriously by the project team or the organization.

Project Management Practice

To keep the person affected by an issue from escalating the situation, a response to being informed of the issue would ideally take one of two forms:

"... thank you for informing us of [the issue].
We are currently investigating and expect to be able to give you a response by not later than [date / time]."

Obviously, a more detailed response must be supplied by the given deadline...

Or

"... Thank you for informing us about [the issue].
We have investigated and identified the cause of the issue.

To resolve the issue we plan to:
[Action 1] to be completed by [Date / time]
[Action 2] to be completed by [Date / time]
...

(If appropriate) We apologize for any inconvenience caused and fully expect that this will resolve [the issue]."

Note: It should be obvious to the customer that the actions will resolve the issue. If not, then the reasons for the actions will need to be explained.

Project Management Practice

If the resolution of the issue will have a significant impact on the project delivery, then either the project manager or the project sponsor will need to be involved.

If it is likely that the issue will escalate, then ensure that the project manager and the project sponsor are informed of the issue and any steps undertaken to resolve it. This will put them in a better position to react in the best interests of everyone involved.

REQUESTS FOR DECISIONS

Making a request for a decision is not part of the regular cycle of tasks that the project manager performs during execution. There should not be a need to ask the project sponsor for decisions on a regular basis during the project lifecycle.

Sometimes, when dealing with issues or change requests related to the project, there is a need to ask the project sponsor for a decision. A decision request is typically made during a steering board meeting. At the steering board meeting, the project manager and the project sponsor are both present to review the project progress. Other major stakeholders may have been invited as well. However, if an urgent decision is required, do not wait for the next steering board meeting.

In general, some preparation will be required when requesting a decision. Remember that while the project sponsor will know the overall goals of the project, they will know less about the project in general and the specific issue itself than the project manager does. In particular, it is highly unlikely that the project sponsor will know the specific details and background that lead to the decision request.

When the project manager makes a request for a decision to the project sponsor, it is important that the project sponsor is supplied sufficient information so that they can actually make the decision. It may sound obvious, but it is surprising how often decision requests are presented that do not contain enough information to allow a decision to be made.

So that a project sponsor can make a decision, they will need to:

- Understand what the issue is
- Understand why this issue cannot be dealt with by the project team / project manager
- Know what the available options are
- Understand the implications of each of the available options.

This may also sound quite obvious, but quite often the issue is not clearly explained, only one option is presented (and it is quite clear that alternatives have not been considered), or the implications of choosing each option are not clear.

Start with a concise description of the issue and explain the circumstances or limitations that have created the issue. It should be self-evident from the description and the implications why the project manager is unable to make this decision or to find a solution within the project team. If it is not self-evident, then be prepared to explain

Project Management Practice

during the steering board meeting why a decision from the steering board is required.

Briefly present the possible options for dealing with the issue. This should include not only a description of the options themselves, but also what the implications of choosing each option are, for both the project and the organization in general.

A recommendation from the project manager on how to solve the issue is generally greeted favorably by a steering board. In this case the project manager should be prepared to explain why the recommended option is their preferred option, as well as accept the decision of the project sponsor gracefully if their recommendation is not followed.

Refer to the slide below for a sample of a decision request template.

Project Management Practice

Sample Decision Request Template

<Project>	Decision Request

Decision Summary

<Summary of the decision requested>

Available Options

<Brief Summary of the available options>

<What is the impact of the available options with regard to the project and/or the organisation as a whole?>

<Optional: Recommendation>

Once the decision is made, it should be documented and implemented as soon as possible.

MANAGEMENT OF THE PROJECT TEAM

An important part of project management during the execution phase of the project is to be able to manage the project team. This skill has become even more important in today's world where many people working together on a project may not sit in the same offices, or even in the same countries.

The project team was quite small during the initiation and planning phases. In the execution and monitoring phase the project manager has the full project team in place. People management skills play a far more important role now than they did during initiation or planning.

If the project has a many people working closely together for a number of months, then it is helpful to be aware of the phases of team development and the possibility of communication issues. The final topic in this section covers some simple techniques for motivating people.

Team Building:

Any team will go through a number of development phases. These phases have been described by Bruce Tuchman's work on organizational development. From a practical point of view, the project manager needs to know these phases so that they are prepared as the project team goes though each of the team's developmental phases.

Project Management Practice

For further details on Bruce Tuchman's work on organizational development phases: Forming, Storming, Norming, Performing, and Adjourning, refer to *Team Building* on page 335 of *Part V Tools*.

The text below does not duplicate the information in *Part V Tools*, instead it concentrates on what the project manager can expect and the likely issues that they will need to deal with.

Forming:

During forming, the project team may feel unsure of themselves or their role in the project. Therefore, it is important to communicate clear goals for both the project as a whole and for each individual project team member in the early phases of project execution.

Storming:

The project manager will need to spend a lot of time managing people during this phase of team development. All sorts of minor issues may be presented as show stoppers. The underlying issue is most likely that the project team is struggling with the new situation and are, for some reason, unhappy. The project manager will need to deal with the minor issues as they come up, but also attempt to identify and resolve the underlying issues as well.

Project Management Practice

Norming:

This is a good time for the project manager to move from simple management (do this, then do that) towards coaching people. Consider the capabilities within the team. Is there anyone who is underutilized? Is there anyone who has the potential to develop the skills necessary for them to take on a new role? Is it possible to make an opportunity within the bounds of the project for them to develop those skills?

Performing:

The project manager should be able to have a more "hands off" approach towards people management during the performing phase. The team is functioning well and the project manager should not need to spend large amounts of time on people management.

Adjourning:

For most small- and medium-sized projects, adjourning is unlikely to be an issue. For larger projects, where the project team has been committed to the project full time for a significant length of time, adjourning may require some thought.

If adjourning is likely to cause issues, then the project manager will need to speak with the line managers of the team members to plan their integration back into normal line work, or into the next project, as smoothly as possible. It will be important that, when the team member is released from the team, they will leave with their work complete and with a new perspective. This will help ease their transition out of the project.

Communication:

With the project in full swing during the execution and monitoring phase, good communication becomes very important. This will be managed via the communication plan.

On a day-to-day basis, it will also be important to recognize that the team members come from very different backgrounds and they may find it difficult to find a common language for communication. The project manager has the job of ensuring that a common level of communication is found. Issues that affect the overall progress need to be understood by the whole team.

Communicating with project stakeholders outside of the core project team needs some thought. A common mistake is to produce a report or newsletter that contains technical details that people outside of the core project team will not understand. The communication needs to be prepared with the receiver of the information in mind. It needs to convey the information regarding progress or issues in a way that can be clearly understood. Ideally, the communication will also make it clear what the implications of this information are.

Project Management Practice

Refer to *Communication* on page 342 of *Part V Tools* for more details on the SMCR communication model. Understanding this can assist in avoiding communication issues.

Motivating People

After Charys, my partner, read the first serious draft of this book, she added a note:

"You haven't included anything about how to kick people's butts. It seems to me that a lot of your time as a PM is spent on just that. Could you add anything helpful about it?"

Hmm. "Kicking butts" is not how I view what I do. However, it does raise a valid point. How do you get people to work for you?

It is absolutely vital, as a project manager, that others will complete the work that you are asking them to complete. Typically, the work that you are asking them to do is competing with work that they are already doing for other project managers or their line manager.

As a project manager, you do not usually have any disciplinary authority over the team that you are working for. Any authority or power that you have comes from the project sponsor. Obviously, you cannot refer everything to the project sponsor every time you have a minor issue.

Project Management Practice

The project sponsor has made you project manager so that you can deal with the project on their behalf.

> **Note:**
>
> Types of Authority and Power on page 333, provides a detailed discussion of the different types of authority and power that a person may have within an organization.

It is worth spending the time to ensure that the project team is motivated and committed to delivering the project. It is also often necessary to gather support for the project with influential stakeholders who are outside of the core project team.

Every project manager develops their own style or methods for motivating their team. Normally it comes down to a carrot and stick approach, with some maneuvering behind the scenes to ensure that you have the support that you need. Here are some ideas...

Ask Nicely...

Do not underestimate the power of asking someone nicely to do the work that needs to be done. Most people genuinely would like to help and will only say "no" if they really do not see a way to help you.

Project Management Practice

Ensure the Project Team is Aware of the Importance of the Project

If the project is important to the organization, then make sure that the project team is aware that the project is important and of the reasons why. Let them know that the work that they are doing is being tracked by the executive team because the executive team is personally interested in the results of this project. Get the project team's support right from the start.

Ensure that the Line Managers of the Project Team are Aware of the Importance of the Project

It is also important to let the project team's line managers know that the project is important and why it is important to the organization.

The project team's line managers are the people most likely to give the project team members work which will compete with the project's work. Get their support as early as possible. Regularly remind the line managers of the importance of the project and the vital work which their team of experts is performing. This will help to keep the team members on the team.

Compare the Overall Project Benefits with the Work Required to Complete Their Work Package

When faced with a refusal to deliver a work package, try comparing the overall benefit of the project to the work involved in delivering the particular work package. As an

Project Management Practice

example, "I understand that you have a lot of work on at the moment. But, the results of this project are expected to save the organization 10 Million over the next two years. Do you really think the management team is going to accept that they will lose those savings because this one work package is not going to be completed?"

Offering a Choice

People like to know that they are important. Sometimes, especially if they feel they have not been taken seriously or have been circumvented, they will block things just to make the point that they have a say, too. This means that something went wrong in the stakeholder management process. If this kind of issue crops up, review what is currently being done to obtain and keep the support of your influential stakeholders.

However, to get past the issue for now, it can be helpful to offer a choice. "To succeed, we have two options. We can either do X or Y but not both. Which would you prefer?" And then implement that solution. The solution may not be perfect, but it will get the project moving again.

Do not Treat a Refusal as a Personal Issue

Most people would prefer to help and do the work that is being asked of them. If they are refusing to do the work, then find out why. In most cases, the reason is that their line manager has told them to work on a different task because that task is more important or more urgent. In general, it should be clear which task is more important, so either the project manager needs to back off or they need to talk to the line manager to explain the priority of the project.

If the relative priorities are not clear, then an escalation will likely be required to get the issue in front of someone who is able to decide which task is most important to the organization. This normally means going up the organization line structure until you have a manager with direct responsibility for everyone involved. Hopefully, this will be the project sponsor. Even if it is not, the relevant manager should be able to make a decision that everyone will accept.

Poor Work Plus Excuses does not Equal Good Work

As a project manager, you need to deliver good results. Excuses may help to understand the reasons why things are not working and provide pointers on how they can be fixed. But delivering poor results with excuses will not be accepted from your project sponsor, so do accept it from others.

If you are fed a line of excuses, listen to them carefully and then ask, "What needs to happen to fix this?" Wherever possible, pick a solution that the person who is making the excuses can implement alone.

Project Management Practice

In some cases, it may be necessary to look deeper. A line of excuses points to the person not wanting to do the task for some reason. There is a lack of motivation. To get the person really active again, it will be necessary to find a way of motivating them.

Focus on Progress When Reporting

The reports that the project manager produces will affect how the project is seen by the team and by other project stakeholders.

If the reports focus on results, then everyone involved with the project will focus on what needs to be done to deliver those results.

It is surprisingly easy to end up producing regular reports that are focused on costs, issues, or some other topic, and not on results. All these other topics are also important and deserve the time of the project manager and the rest of the project team. But, to deliver the project successfully, the main focus needs to be kept on producing the desired results.

Project Management Practice

CHAPTER 17.

PROJECT CLOSURE

All good things come to an end…!

The execution phase of the project has delivered everything that the project was created to deliver, so now it is time to close the project down.

Project closure completes all the remaining tasks necessary to finalize the project. This includes:

- Formal handover and acceptance from the project sponsor
- A lessons learned session
- Formal project closure
- Administrative Tasks

Formal Handover and Acceptance from the Project Sponsor

Project handover is when the project deliverables (product sample, product documentation, process documentation, project documentation, etc.) are put together in one sensible package and presented to the project sponsor. It is normal to organize a meeting to take the project sponsor through the complete package and answer any questions that may arise.

If there is an external customer involved, the project sponsor may request that the project manager present the successfully completed project to the customer. More often, the project sponsor will hand over the completed results to the customer.

The project sponsor (and the customer if there is one) will formally accept the project results. Some organizations, particularly if a customer is receiving the project results, may require a signature to recognize that the project results have been accepted. Other organizations may be less formal and a simple e-Mail may suffice.

Ensure that a copy of any relevant documentation is stored in the central project repository.

Project Management Practice

LESSONS LEARNED

The main purpose of a lessons learned session is to ensure that the knowledge gained by the project team does not get lost. Instead, it is made available to the organization as a whole for future use.

Some projects generate so much new knowledge and so many processes improvements that it is worth gathering and documenting the lessons learned throughout the entire project.

Some lessons learned are sufficiently important that they should be discussed with the project sponsor at a steering board meeting during execution. For most projects, it is sufficient to note the lessons learned and have them reviewed and presented together at the end of the project.

When reviewing the lessons learned with the project team, the project sponsor will be looking for opportunities to help the organization in addition to knowledge that would assist similar projects in the future. It is not unusual for output from these sessions to enable significant improvements to be made in how the organization completes their normal operational tasks.

A lessons learned session typically covers three main topics:

Project Management Practice

- A review of the time estimates provided
- Identify things which went well that the organization could benefit from in the future
- Identify things which went badly, with suggestions regarding how these could possibly be avoided in the future

Review Time Estimates

Being able to create good time estimates is a very useful skill to develop within the organization. It will help to ensure that the workload for future projects can be predicted accurately. Estimation is a skill that improves with practice and good feedback. Therefore, it is helpful to everyone who provided estimates during planning to be given a feedback on the actual time taken to complete the tasks that they estimated.

Take the time estimates that you created yourself, or were given, and compare them to the actual time that the task took.

Make it very clear that the feedback is being given to everyone involved and that the reason for doing so is to improve the organization's ability to provide good budget estimates for project work.

The Lessons Learned Session

Most of the project team will consider the formal handover to the project sponsor (and/or customer) as being their final involvement in the project. Motivating the team to come together for a final lessons learned session can sometimes be a challenge. The team considers the project closed and will have moved on to other work. If your organization is prepared to sponsor some kind of celebration for completing the project, then it is a good idea to hold the lessons learned session at the same time. Gather the feedback, then go out and celebrate.

Even if your organization is not able to fund an end of project celebration (or the project is too small to warrant one), then still make the effort to hold a meeting with all the team members and capture their feedback on the project.

Start by asking the project team for feedback on what went well. Can any of these be used as "best practice" examples for the future?

Next, ask the project team for feedback regarding what went badly. What recommendations can be made to help other people in the organization avoid having the same difficulties? How can things be improved? Take care to finish the whole session on as positive a note as possible.

Project Management Practice

Review the findings of the lessons learned session with your project sponsor and the rest of the steering board. If the lessons learned are presented in a constructive manner with recommendations or at least ideas as to how things can be improved in the future, then most good project sponsors are grateful for the feedback and are eager to implement improvement within the organization.

If the project sponsor does decide to follow up on the recommendations out of a lessons learned session, then feedback should be given to the team, to let them know that their ideas are being acted on.

Store the documents from the lessons learned session in the central project repository. Anyone performing a similar project in the future will be very interested to know the improvements that this project team recommended.

FORMAL PROJECT CLOSURE

The project has been completed. Well done!

A successfully completed project is a reason for a celebration. Go and enjoy a night out. You and your project team have earned it!

Success Story

The world in which we work is often filled with information about things that have gone wrong. Managers, in particular, are often faced with a constant stream of issues that need their attention.

The project has been finished. This means that the organization has completed something new, something to be proud of. So, tell the organization (and anyone else who might be interested) that this good work has been successfully completed. People will be interested to know.

Write a few short statements explaining what the project has achieved and what the benefits to the organization are, or what the benefits to the organization's customers are. Forward this written statement to your line manager or to the project sponsor for inclusion in the regular management reports.

Project Management Practice

Thank Your Team

Take the time to thank each member of the team for their work on the project. Remember, without your team, the project would never have been completed. A word of thanks is fully justified and will help you to win their support for your next project.

ADMINISTRATIVE TASKS

There are normally some minor administrative tasks which need to be completed as the project closes. These will often include the following:

- Check that the project documentation is complete
- Check that everyone involved has charged all their costs or hours worked to the project cost code
- Close the cost code for the project
- Inform the PMO that the project is now closed and inactive. The PMO will:
  - Ensure that the project is removed from the list of active projects
  - Update the relevant central risk register to remove any remaining risks which are still listed as open for the project
  - Ensure that the central project documentation is frozen and made generally available for future reference
  - In some cases, the PMO may decide to audit the project to ensure that the organization's project management standards have been kept

CLOSING FAILED OR INCOMPLETE PROJECTS

Sometimes projects fail. In fact, various studies show that approximately a third of all projects fail to meet the original business goal and less than 40% of projects are delivered on time and within budget. Hopefully, by applying the stripped down project management methodology, you and your organization will be able to avoid many of the pitfalls which await unprepared project managers.

The reasons that a project fails are varied. The most frequent causes of failure are:

- Budget overrun.
- This is most often caused by either:
  o an overly optimistic initial project plan
  o insufficient initial planning
- An unexpected issue during execution provided a large enough obstacle that the project needed to be abandoned
- Not enough support within the organization, or from the customer, to complete the project.
- This normally shows up when project team members are regularly removed from the project to deal with other, higher priority, tasks

Project Management Practice

Whatever the reason, the project needs to be closed without delivering the expected benefits which the project was intended to deliver.

Goal when Closing Failed Projects:

If a project fails and needs to be closed as incomplete, then the overall goal during closure is to manage the closure in such a way that the organization obtains the maximum possible benefit from the results that were achieved.

To obtain the maximum value from a failed project, the organization will want to get the most out of any partial results achieved, and also to know what mistakes were made so that these are not repeated in the future.

Identify Value for the Organization

Examine the work packages and deliverables that the project was intended to deliver. Are any of the completed work packages or completed deliverables valuable to the organization or the customer? If the answer is yes, prepare the completed work packages and deliverables for a partial handover to the project sponsor.

The project sponsor will want to use these results to show that even though the project failed, the organization and /

Project Management Practice

or the customer still received some value or benefit from the project.

Next, examine the partially completed work packages and deliverables. The project manager and the project sponsor will need to decide if there is any value in completing some of the outstanding work packages and deliverables even though not all the remaining work packages will be completed.

Identify What Went Wrong

Hold a lessons learned session to identify where the project went wrong and what can be done in the future to avoid similar mistakes.

When holding the lessons learned session, keep in mind that even though the major focus will be on avoiding similar mistakes in the future, there also may have been some things that the project did well. These things also need to be captured for future use.

Project Management Practice

Part V

Tools

This tools section brings together some tools that could be helpful to manage a project. No project will require all of these tools, but all projects could benefit by the use of at least some of these tools.

The tools presented in stripped down project management are aimed at helping project managers to be as effective as possible. For each tool, there is a short introduction stating when and why the tool could be helpful. If more than one tool is presented for a particular task, there is an explanation of which tool would be best under which circumstances. Select and use the tools that are most appropriate for the task at hand.

CHAPTER 18.

CREATIVITY

Projects are all about innovation, so expect creativity to play a role in most projects. There is a tendency to associate creativity with some kind of divine inspiration, or think of it as a talent that is restricted to very small pool of exceptional people. In fact, everyone is creative in some way. The challenge is to discover how to tap into that creative potential.

If there is an interest in promoting creativity in yourself or within your organization, then it is often helpful to put creativity and innovation into a framework. Once in a framework, it is far simpler to create a process around it that everyone can follow and contribute to.

There are quite a few frameworks available for creativity. The ones which are likely to be of the most use in a project environment are ones which have a clear step-by-step process, such as Osborn's Classic Brainstorming, the Buffalo Six Phase Method, or RAND Corporation's Classic Systems Analysis.

Looking at the elements of these process oriented frameworks, it becomes clear that they all share common factors. Refer to the diagram on the next page, which

Tools

gathers together the main process steps from the frameworks mentioned above.

Creativity Framework

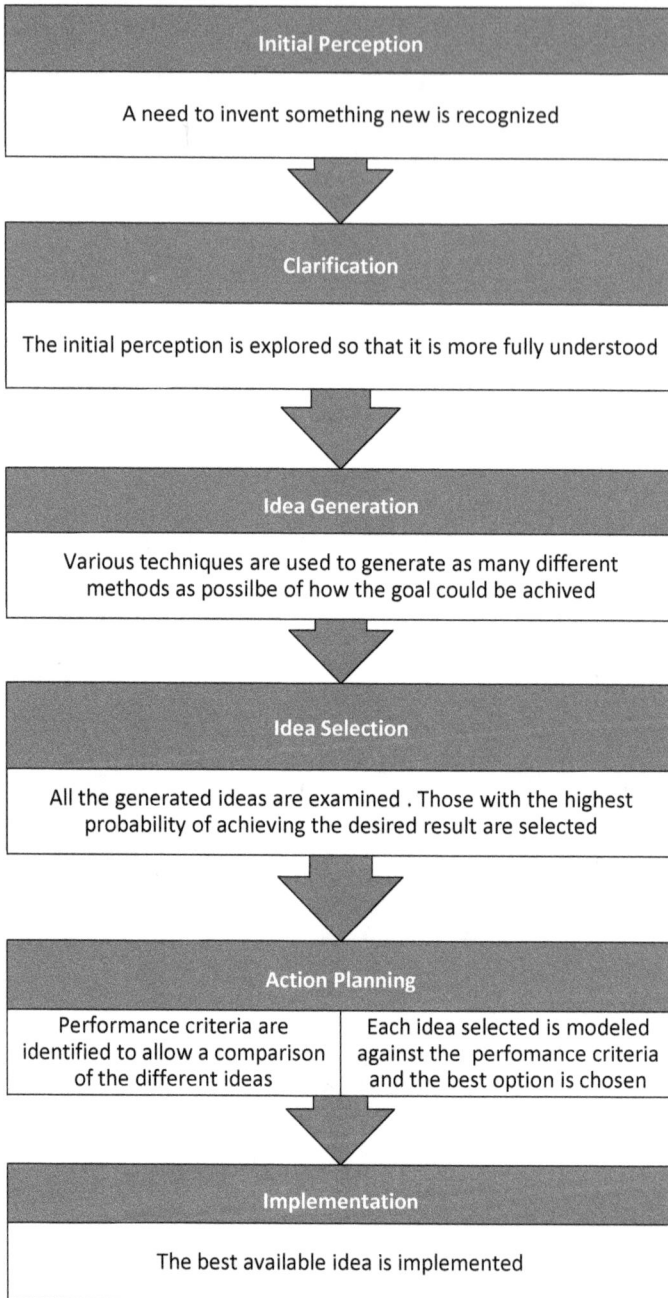

Initial Perception

A need to invent something new is recognized

Clarification

The initial perception is explored so that it is more fully understood

Idea Generation

Various techniques are used to generate as many different methods as possilbe of how the goal could be achived

Idea Selection

All the generated ideas are examined . Those with the highest probability of achieving the desired result are selected

Action Planning

Performance criteria are identified to allow a comparison of the different ideas	Each idea selected is modeled against the perfomance criteria and the best option is chosen

Implementation

The best available idea is implemented

Tools

Putting creativity into this kind of framework takes it away from the realm of inspired genius and places it firmly into the kind of day to day work which we all do.

Initial Perception

Initial perception is the simple realization that something new needs to be developed. The idea often comes from the necessity of solving an issue, but it can come from almost anything. This is the part of the creative process that may actually have a factor of "inspiration" in it. In general, the need for a solution is obvious to almost anyone actively looking to make improvements in the chosen area.

Clarification

Before investing any serious amount of time or effort into finding a creative solution for something, it is important to clarify exactly what the solution should achieve.

The results of the later phases of the creative process will be far more productive if the overall goal is well defined.

Clarification: The Invention of the Sewing Machine

The earliest attempts to create a machine that could sew failed. Those early inventors attempted to duplicate the complex movements that a seamstress made when moving a needle and thread to sew two pieces of cloth together.

Tools

In the early phases of industrialization, it was realized that the goal was not to replicate the movements that a person made while sewing. The goal was to join two pieces of cloth together using thread. Once the various inventors of sewing machines around the world realized this, the first real progress on creating a sewing machine was made.

For additional tools to assist with clarification, refer to the section *Applying 5W's and one H* (Who? Why? What? Where? When? How?) on page 268.

Idea Generation

The part of creative thinking that many of us find hardest is idea generation. Normally the problem is clear, but how should it be solved? The cognitive part of the human brain will attempt to reuse the paths that have led to successful solutions in the past. When these paths fail, it can be difficult for us to come up with an alternative path to a solution. We feel "lost in the woods".

By using tools such as the ones listed below, it is possible to help the brain move away from the paths of past solutions and onto new paths. This makes it possible to get a new viewpoint on the desired result, and a new viewpoint will often bring new ideas of how to reach a solution.

Tools

Methods for idea generation can include:

- Brainstorming (See page 262)
- Mind Mapping (See page 264)
- Reversal: Examining how to make something worse may provide productive insight on how to make something better. (See page 267)

Idea Selection

Having generated a number of ideas, the next step is to select those ideas that are most likely to achieve the desired goal. Some ideas can be thrown out as clearly unworkable. They were an important part of the creative process in that they may have led to other, more workable, ideas. However now, they are no longer needed.

If one idea is the sole possibility of success, then it is possible to jump directly to the implementation phase. In most cases though, a short list of ideas is created, each of which has advantages and disadvantages. These ideas can be taken into the next step, "action planning".

Action Planning

The first step in action planning is to review the results of the clarification step. Based on the results of the clarification step, performance criteria are created. These

Tools

criteria will be used to judge the different methods of reaching the desired solution.

Let use buying a car as a metaphor for selecting an idea to be used to achieve the desired solution. All cars have the same basic function: They take the driver and any passenger from where they are now to where they want to go. But, if it is so simple, why are so many different cars available? Each person will have their own selection criteria and will weight those selection criteria according to their own personal needs. Possible criteria for selecting a car could include:

- Budget
- Safety record
- Running costs
- How much can it carry
- How well does the car fit our self image

Each person looking for the best method of finding a solution to the problem at hand will also use different selection criteria.

Once the selection criteria have been identified, a way of modeling the advantages and disadvantages of the ideas against each other is required. The model chosen will be specific to the case at hand. It could be a simple score card or the result of a complex financial calculation. The sole goal of the model is to compare the ideas against each other and select the best idea from them.

Implementation

Having decided on the best idea or method of achieving the desired solution, the final step is to follow up and implement the idea.

Tools

BRAINSTORMING

The goal of brainstorming is to create as many ideas on a particular topic as possible in a short space of time.

Brainstorming involves letting the brain freely associate on a particular topic and then capturing all the different ideas that occur. Once all the ideas have been captured, it is often useful to look at each of the ideas in more detail and see if these spark any additional ideas. After this second (and if helpful, subsequent) round has completed, then it is time to look at the ideas critically to identify which ones are of real use to the purpose at hand.

Ideally, a brainstorming session includes a small group of people. This makes it possible for an idea from one person to inspire other members of the group to further ideas.

The following rules apply during the actual brainstorming phase:

- No criticism of any idea. Even the silliest or craziest ideas can be the stepping stone to a workable solution
- No evaluation of the idea
  Starting evaluation pulls the brain away from the creative process of coming up with possible alternative solutions

- Combining and expanding on other people's ideas is to be encouraged

When running a brain storming session, you will need to:

- Make sure that all the ideas are captured and written down
- Keep the actual time quite short. After 5-15 minutes the ideas will probably start to dry up.
- Once the ideas stop flowing, more on to the review and evaluation phase
- If possible, create a fun, jokey atmosphere.
  The more relaxed people are, the easier they will find it to present their ideas

If you are running a brain storming session with people who have not done this before, or are feeling nervous, then it can be a good idea to have a warm up session first. Try putting a plastic cup in the middle of the table and ask everyone to come up with as many uses for the plastic cup as possible.

Tools

MIND MAPPING

Mind mapping is a simple, yet surprisingly powerful tool for examining complex questions.

Mind mapping uses diagram techniques to pull all the factors related to a topic together onto one page and to show some of the relationships between them. This technique is particularly useful if you are going round in circles and can't seem to break out.

To draw a mind map:

- Start off by stating the subject as clearly as possible in the middle of the page. Put a circle round it
- For each major factor or component related to the subject, draw a line off of the subject in the middle and label it
- Examine each major factor or component in turn. For each sub-factor or sub-component draw a line off of the major factor or component and label it. Feel free to jump between topics as different ideas occur
- Repeat this until all the relevant factors or components have been represented on the page
- If two topics in different branches are linked, connect them with a (dotted) line

There are software-based mind mapping tools available. These can be helpful when working in a group, or if there is a need to present the results of the mind map to a larger group. When working alone, most people prefer to sketch the mind map on a piece of paper.

Refer to the diagram on the next page for an example of a mind map on the topic of increasing the profitability of an organization.

Example of a Mind Map

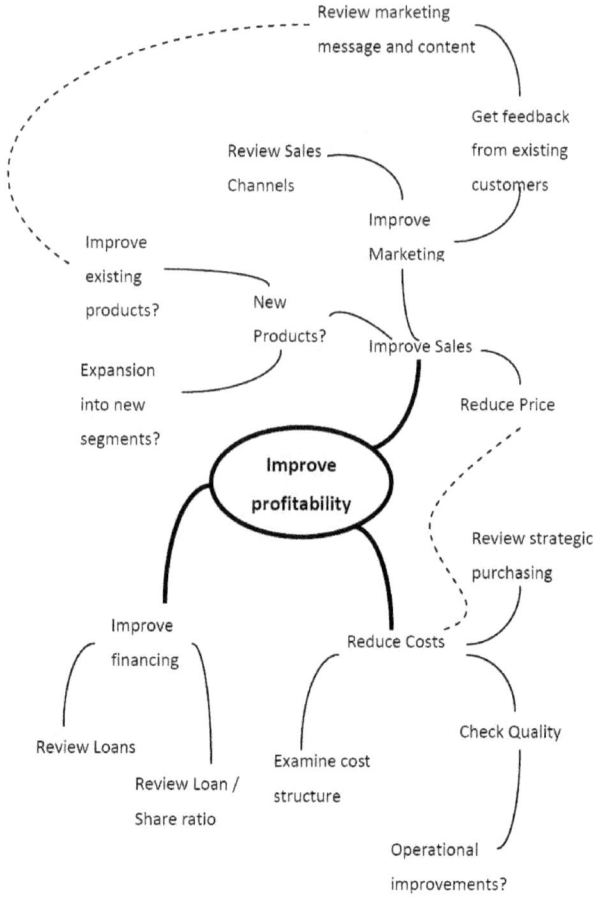

REVERSAL:

Reversal can be a useful tool for getting fresh ideas or for identifying the most important factors on a topic.

With reversal, instead of reaching directly for the desired result, investigate what would need to be done to achieve the opposite of the desired result. This can provide a new perspective on how to achieve the original goal.

For example, let us say that a project has the goal of improving the production of a particular product. The team is tired and have run out of ideas. Ask the team to take a short break and then ask them to come up with ideas on how to make the production worse. These can give valuable pointers on how to improve the situation. In some cases, it may even be recognized that some of the ways to make production worse are actually in place right now.

An extension of reversal is to use a "double reversal". In other words, to ask a question such as "How do I avoid the opposite of what I am trying to achieve?" Here is an example to help explain the idea: For most people, the answers to "How do I get rich?" and "How do I avoid becoming bankrupt?" are quite different. However, answering the question "How do I avoid becoming bankrupt?" may provide some useful pointers towards realistically solving the question "How do I get rich?"

Tools

APPLYING 5W'S AND ONE H

The 5W's and one H are: Who? Why? What? Where? When? and How?

They are used as a check that all the most important aspects of a new development have been examined.

Rudyard Kipling included the 5W's and one H in a poem, which was contained in his story "The Elephant's Child". It was published as part of the "Just So Stories" in 1902.

Problem analysis using this method is sometimes referred to as the "Kipling Method".

The 5W's and one H are normally referred to in the context of journalism and police investigations. In these contexts, they are considered to be the required formula to getting the complete story on a topic. Similarly, these questions can be usefully applied to research on any almost any new development:

- Who would want to use this product or service?
- Why would they want to use it?
- What is the benefit that they would gain by using it?
- Where would they use it?

- When would they use it?
- How would they use it?

Answering these six questions provides a good understanding of what the new development should achieve. This in turn provides a good overview of the most important features which the new product or service would need to include.

CHAPTER 19.

THE PROJECT MANAGEMENT TRIANGLE

The project management triangle is intended to help project managers remember to look for all the possible options when dealing with a project constraint.

Any project has constraints. It has a limited budget, limited resources, a limited time frame for delivery, and the results are expected to achieve a particular level of quality. The project management triangle is a model that can be used to represent or analyze the constraints existing on a project.

The Project Management Triangle

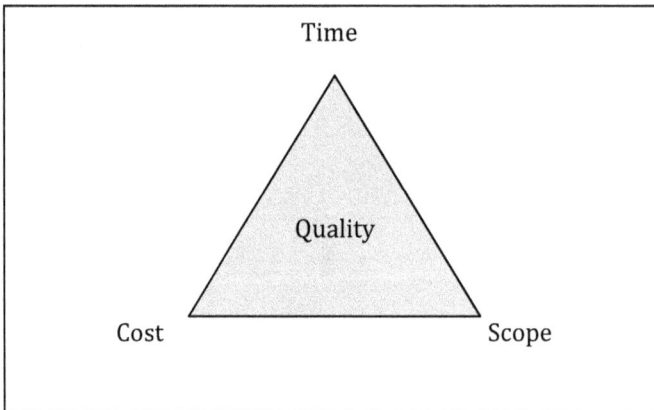

Time

Quality

Cost

Scope

The project management triangle model states that the constraints time, scope, cost, and quality cannot be changed independently. A change in one constraint will have an impact on the other constraints.

The project management triangle is used either during the planning phase or during the execution and monitoring phase to create options for dealing with constraints.

During planning, the tool is mainly used to ensure that the project scope meets the available time, budget and quality expectations. It is often helpful to examine each constraining factor (delivery deadline, available budget, required features or deliverables, and expected level of quality) individually, then systematically check each of the other factors against it.

During execution, the project management triangle is used when an issue has occurred which creates a new constraint on the project. This tool is helpful in generating options for what could be done to reduce the impact of the new constraint.

For example, if a project is starting to exceed the available budget, then cost is the new constraining factor. Some options to counter this may be:

- Time: Extend the time required to deliver the expected project results. Doing so may allow the available resources to be reduced. In turn, this may reduce the overall cost of the project.

- Quality: The quality of some work packages may only have a minimal effect on the final delivered results. Reducing the quality of those work packages may free up sufficient funds to allow the project to complete successfully.

- Scope: Reduce the overall scope of the project to focus on the most important deliverables. Reducing the scope will free up funds for the project.

Tools

CHAPTER 20.

WORK BREAKDOWN STRUCTURE

A work breakdown structure (WBS) is an excellent tool to decompose a larger, more complex project into a set of manageable work packages.

To use a WBS, start with the project itself. Then, underneath the project name, list the main project deliverables. Each of the project deliverables needs to be broken down into smaller and smaller pieces until the level of the smallest work package is created. Ideally, a single work package should be a piece of work that can be completed by a single person or single team of experts in a reasonable amount of time. Refer to the diagram below for an example of a WBS.

Work Breakdown Structure

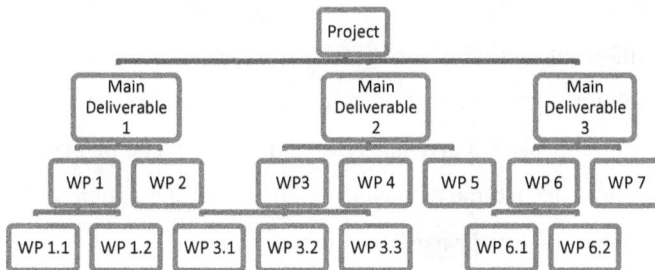

The advantage of having a WBS instead of just a plain list of work packages is that it easier to identify how each individual work package fits together to create the entire project.

It also provides automatic checkpoints as the project progresses to ensure that project results are being fully delivered and nothing is missed. For example, when WP 1.1 and WP 1.2 are completed, then WP 1 should be fully complete. When WP 3, WP 4, and WP 5 are complete, then the Main Deliverable 2 should be fully complete. If not, then something has been missed or otherwise gone wrong. Implementing regular checkpoints helps make sure that issues are discovered early, and not during the closing phase of the project.

Another advantage of using a WBS is that one person can decompose a single main deliverable or major work package into more detailed work packages. This person can work independently of anyone else working on a different section of the WBS. The structure of the WBS also allows each person to retain a complete overview of the whole project. Particularly for larger projects, or projects where a third party is contracted to complete some of the tasks, this is very useful.

A WBS tends to encourage a very short description of the individual work packages. This can lead to scope slip as different people will have different understandings of the intended content of the work package. (Remember that the WBS will be created at an early phase of planning before the detailed work package descriptions have been finalized.) To help avoid this, it can be useful to take the WBS and turn it into a list format. This allows for a more detailed description of the intent of the work package. This format can also be used as an Action Item List (AIL) to help track progress through the project.

Compare the example of the WBS taken from beginning of this section with the one below, which is in AIL format. Note the extra detail that has been added while retaining the basic structure of the original WBS. The disadvantage of having the WBS in this form is that it is more difficult to see the overall structure of the project.

WBS in AIL Format

Improve IT Service Delivery					
Work Pckg.	Short description	Rsp.	Start	End	Status
MD 1	Reduce the total number of user incidents by 50%	Mark	1. Jun.	13. Jul.	
WP 1	Analyse user incidents over the past 3 months	Alan	1. Jun.	15. Jun.	
WP 1.1	Identify the most frequent incidents	Claire	1. Jun.	8. Jun.	

Improve IT Service Delivery					
Work Pckg.	Short description	Rsp.	Start	End	Status
WP 1.2	Identify the root cause of the incidents and deliver a proposal on how it could be solved permanently	Peter	8. Jun.	15. Jun.	
WP 2	Implement the solutions necessary to resolve the recurring incidents permanently	Peter	15. Jun.	13. Jul.	
MD 2	Review Delivery Capacity	Tobi	1. Jun.	15. Jun.	
WP 3	Produce capacity review for all infrastructure	Gary	1. Jun.	15. Jun.	
WP 3.1	Produce capacity review for network components. Identify areas which are likely to become an issue over the next three months.	Peter	1. Jun.	15. Jun.	
WP 3.2	Produce capacity review for storage components. Identify areas that are likely to become an issue over the next three	Gary	1. Jun.	15. Jun.	

Improve IT Service Delivery					
Work Pckg.	Short description	Rsp.	Start	End	Status
	months.				
WP 3.3	Produce capacity review for server components. Identify areas which are likely to become an issue over the next three months.	Kate	1. Jun.	15. Jun.	
WP 4	Review helpdesk capacity. In particular, what are the peak times and the incident response time SLAs being kept	Alan	1. Jun.	8. Jun.	
WP 5	Review System Administrator capacity. In particular, how many open incidents & problems are there and is the SLA for incident response being adhered to?	Kate	1. Jun.	8. Jun.	
MD 3	Review processes	Keith	1. Jun.	29. Jun.	

Tools

Improve IT Service Delivery					
Work Pckg.	Short description	Rsp.	Start	End	Status
WP 6	Review Incident Process.	Alan	8. Jun.	29. Jun.	
WP 6.1	Incident process: are the documented processes being followed in practice? If not, why not?	Ginger	8. Jun.	22. Jun.	
WP 6.2	Gather input from all people involved. Can the documented procedures be improved? If so, how?	Ginger	8. Jun.	29. Jun.	
WP 7	Review Order Process.	Rob	1. Jun.	29. Jun.	

When using an AIL in a meeting, do not attempt to cover too many action points. About 5-7 is a good number to aim for. If you are regularly covering more than 12-15 points in a meeting, then look at restructuring the meeting. Split the meeting into several smaller meetings, each with a smaller group of people. This will make your meetings more productive. An example of this would be to hold separate meetings to discuss the open points for each single major deliverable, instead of one large meeting for the whole project team.

CHAPTER 21.

ESTIMATING TECHNIQUES

Accurately estimating the cost and effort involved in a project can be extremely difficult. There will not necessarily be much experience for the organization to draw on when estimating the time and resources required for the project.

That having been said, most projects will build on the competencies that the organization has already developed. Therefore, the organization is likely to have experience with some or possibly even most of the tasks that need to be completed.

Regardless of the estimating techniques that are used within the organization, estimation is a skill that improves with practice and feedback. Make sure that anyone who regularly provides work estimates also gets a feedback regarding how accurate their estimate was.

Estimating techniques can be split into general types: "top down" and "bottom up".

Top Down estimating techniques look at the project or major deliverables as a whole. The smaller tasks required complete the project are not examined in any kind of detail.

Tools

Bottom up estimating techniques examine each individual work package. The results from each package are then added together to provide a total estimate for the whole project.

It is a good idea to use both a top down and a bottom up estimating technique. The two different estimation types provide a cross check on each other.

Tools

Top Down Estimating

The following estimating techniques are usually used to provide a top down estimate of the whole project. Top down estimating techniques do not look at the specific details of individual tasks. Instead the the project as a whole is looked at. Estimates are then created for time, cost and resources.

Top down estimating methods are especially useful during initiation and the early planning phases of the project. A top down estimate for the project can normally be provided quite quickly, even if not all the project details are known or agreed. This provides the project sponsor with a guideline regarding the investment required to complete a project before detailed planning is performed.

ANALOGOUS ESTIMATION

Analogous estimation is a top down estimating method. It is probably one of the quickest, simplest and, to be honest, most reliable methods of estimating the time or effort required for completing a piece of work. It is most often used during project initiation to estimate the entire project effort. However, it can just as effectively be applied to individual work packages during the planning phase as well.

The project or work package under consideration is compared to other similar projects or work packages which the organization has performed in the past. By making small adjustments to reflect the differences between the task at hand and previous work, a good first estimate of the total effort, cost and time required to complete the task can be made.

This method works well, if the organization has collected data on previous projects or work packages that are similar to the one presently under consideration.

Tools

DELPHI METHOD

The Delphi Method is a top down estimation method usually used for estimating the time and resources required to complete whole projects or major deliverables rather than individual work packages.

The Delphi Method attempts to resolve the disadvantages of using a single expert to estimate the time and resources for the whole project by gathering estimates from a panel of experts. This method provides more reliable estimates than expert estimation does. It also ensures that a rationale is provided upon which the estimation was based. The drawback is that this method takes considerably longer to complete than using a single expert would. Refer to *Expert* Estimation on page 290 for more details on expert estimation.

This method can be very useful if the organization is attempting something far outside of their current fields of expertise, or something that is considerably larger or more complex than anything that the organization has previously attempted. It is, however, probably overkill for most small to medium projects and normally takes too long for organizations that have a strong focus on time to market and are looking for quick results.

Tools

In the Delphi method, each participant in the panel of experts provides an estimate of the cost and work involved. They also state the rationale for their estimate.

All the results are collected and made available to everyone taking part on the panel. It is to be expected that there will be quite large differences between the estimations produced in the first round.

After reading all the different reasons for the estimates the other experts provided, the experts revise their own estimates. These new estimates will take into account the feedback provided by the other experts on the panel. The second round of estimates are then collected and distributed to the members of the panel again.

After the second and subsequent rounds of estimation, the estimates typically converge. Once the different estimates are reasonably close to each other, the process can stop.

Central to this method is the anonymity of each of the participants in the estimating process. This is necessary to ensure that the panel members do not follow the lead of a senior, or greatly respected, expert who is taking part. Having everyone follow the lead of a senior person on the panel destroys the value of having a panel of people with different opinions, strengths, and experience.

Tools

PARAMETRIC ESTIMATING

Parametric estimating is appropriate in industries or situations where the costs and resources required to complete a project can be estimated quite accurately based on simple metrics or rules of thumb.

The most frequently quoted example is the cost of constructing a house or other building. This can often be estimated quite accurately when the interior volume of the building is known and allowances are made for the standard of the interior fittings. (The architect who created the plans for my house used this method. The results were accepted by the bank and the construction companies involved, and were proven to be quite accurate once the house was completed.)

Other metrics are sometimes used in other industries to estimate either entire projects or particular tasks. They are normally quite accurate since they are based on the results of a large number of organizations within a particular industry performing similar tasks. In fact, if they are not working, perhaps one should ask why...

A word of warning regarding using this method: Parametric estimating makes no allowance for special conditions regarding the actual project being undertaken.

Tools

Example: It cost x Mil to build the last bridge. The next bridge is 10% larger so it will cost approx 10% more to build than the last one. However, this does not allow for factors such as:

- The site where the bridge is being built presents particular challenges
- A bridge which is 10% longer may require different construction techniques to meet the extended span

BOTTOM UP ESTIMATING

Bottom up estimating involves estimating the costs and effort involved in each work package and then adding them all up to provide a total cost for the project.

Bottom up estimation will normally provide a far more accurate estimate of the actual cost and effort involved to complete the whole project than a top-down approach.

It is best to have the time and effort to deliver each work package estimated by the people who are responsible for executing the tasks. This improves accuracy considerably and creates a sense of responsibility during execution for delivering the results on time and with the agreed budget and resources.

The advantage of bottom up estimating is that individual work packages are easier to estimate accurately than entire projects. A single work package is likely to be fully understood by the relevant expert who is doing the estimation. The expert, or responsible team lead, probably has a lot of experience at completing similar tasks. By comparison, it is very rare that one person has experience with, or fully understands, all the work packages in a project. Therefore, it is to be expected that top down estimates of a whole project will be less accurate than estimates of single work packages.

Tools

The disadvantages are:

- It is time consuming to produce the large number of individual estimates that are required
- Some work packages may have content that is completely new to the organization. This will make estimation especially difficult.
- There may be a tendency for the person responsible for delivering the work package to add a certain amount of padding to ensure that the work can be completed within the stated budget or time frame.

This last point, adding padding, needs to be watched for. The cumulative effect of this may be to inflate the total project estimate unreasonably so that the entire project is seen as being too expensive. This can lead to perfectly viable projects being stopped before they reach the execution phase. To counter this, it is often helpful to reassure the experts providing the work package estimates that allowance will be made in the overall project budget for unforeseen circumstances.

Checking the bottom up estimates against the results of a top down estimate will provide a reality check on the overall estimates provided.

Tools

EXPERT ESTIMATION

Expert estimation is normally used to estimate the cost and effort of a single work package that is similar to the work that the expert usually performs. It is probably the most frequently used estimating technique. It can also be used to provide an estimate for the delivery of a whole project.

Expert estimation requires that you have an expert available for the topic in question. The expert will most ideally already work within the organization, but could also be a consultant brought in specifically to support the cost estimation of the project.

The expert will then provide their best estimate of the costs and effort involved in completing the task at hand, based on their understanding of the project requirements and the capabilities of the organization.

Assuming that the relevant expertise is available, this method will often provide an estimate quite quickly. The accuracy of the results is entirely dependent upon how experienced the expert is at providing cost estimates and their knowledge of the capabilities of the organization.

If using an outside consultant, note that one organization may take a considerably different amount of time to

Tools

complete a project than another because they have quite different processes in place to complete the work.

A problem with this method is that, often, the expert cannot provide a rationale for the estimate. This makes it relatively easy for the estimate to be challenged. In practice, the estimates provided by different experts can differ widely.

This method works best when the expert creating the estimation of time and effort is the line manager of the skill area responsible for delivering that work package. The line manager has a thorough understanding of the organization, processes, and of the capabilities of their own team.

Tools

THREE POINT ESTIMATION

For tasks or work packages which contain a lot of variables or unknowns, estimation may be particularly challenging. This can lead to intensive discussion about what a "reasonable" estimate is.

An approach which often resolves this discussion and leads to quite reliable results in practice is called three point estimation.

Three point estimation works as follows:

- Create an optimistic estimate. Call it O.
- Create a most likely estimate. Call it M.
- Create a pessimistic estimate. Call it P

Calculate the estimated time or cost for completion as:

$$Estimate = \frac{(O + 4M + P)}{6}$$

Tip:

Working out the reasons for the differences between the most optimistic estimate and the most pessimistic estimate will often provide good ideas regarding the risks which are related to this particular work package.

Tools

If appropriate, consider including output from the discussion regarding the reasons behind the different estimates into the project's risk register.

CHAPTER 22.

PROJECT SCHEDULE

There are many different methods and tools for creating a project schedule. Two of the methods most often used are described below. When considering which methods and tools to use to develop the project schedule, you should consider the following factors:

- Ease of use
- Readability
- Maintainability

If the project schedule is difficult to read and understand, then the project manager will waste lots of time explaining to other stakeholders how the schedule is intended be used. Instead, it should be a simple tool to help control and report progress.

A project schedule that is difficult to maintain will cost a lot of time and effort that could be put to better use on other project tasks. Therefore, when deciding how the project schedule will be maintained, consider how often the project schedule will need to be updated and how much effort will be involved in updating it.

These days there are many excellent pieces of software available that significantly ease the job of maintaining a

Tools

project schedule. Once the initial project schedule has been entered into the software, changes can be made quite easily to reflect what actually happened during project execution. This makes it much easier to catch delays early and to spot possible ways to improve project performance.

Note that with both of the methods described below (Network Diagrams and Gantt Charts), it is easy to make the assumption that the necessary resources are either available or can be made available. This may not be the case. Ensure that resource availability is checked and any necessary allowances are made in the completed delivery schedule.

Better software packages, intended for creating and maintaining project schedules throughout a project's lifecycle, will enable resources to be defined to the project schedule. It may also be possible to enter planned absences for project team members into the chosen tool. In this case, if a work package needs to be rescheduled, then the software will automatically make allowances for resource availability when creating the updated plan. These tools are not perfect, but they can reduce a lot of the workload involved in maintaining a project schedule and a resource plan.

Tools

TASK DEPENDENCIES

Before we take a closer look at Network Diagrams and Gantt Charts, let's first look at the different types of dependencies which can exist between different project tasks.

No Dependency

The two tasks can be performed completely independently of each other. Independent tasks could be completed in parallel or one after the other in any particular order. An example would be reading a book and taking a bath.

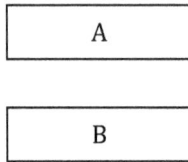

```
┌─────────────────┐
│        A        │
└─────────────────┘

┌─────────────────┐
│        B        │
└─────────────────┘
```

Finish-to-Start

The previous task must complete before the dependent task can start. Finish-to-start dependencies are the most common form of dependency found in project planning.

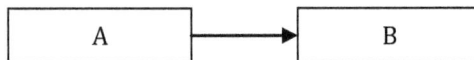

```
┌───────────┐      ┌───────────┐
│     A     │─────▶│     B     │
└───────────┘      └───────────┘
```

For example, a cake must be mixed before it can be baked and must be baked before it can be eaten. (Of course, our kids like to eat the batter before the cake is baked, but that is a different story...)

Tools

Start-to-Start

One task must start before the dependent task may start. Start-to-start dependencies typically include a short time lag to allow the first step of the first task to complete so that the corresponding first step of the second task can be completed.

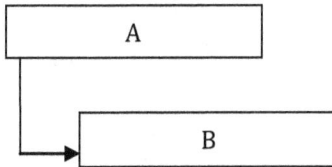

An example would be of laying a long cable underground across the whole country. You have three tasks: Dig a trench. Lay the cable in the trench. Fill in the trench.

In a start-to-finish dependency, you would dig a trench all the way across country. Once that task had been completed, the cable would be laid. Finally the task to fill the trench back in again would start.

A start-to-start dependency would be far more practical: In a start-to-start dependency, the trench would be dug. However, once a reasonable section of the trench had been dug, the cable would be laid into the trench, and the part of the trench in which the cable lay would be filled. The three tasks would run in parallel, each task slightly lagging behind the other, until the entire cable had been laid.

Tools

Finish-to-Finish

One task must finish before the dependent task may finish.

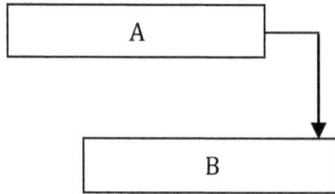

An example of a finish-to-finish dependency would be of documentation that could not complete until testing of the prototype or new development had completed.

Start-to-Finish

This is included for completeness but is rarely required. The first task needs to start before the dependent task can finish.

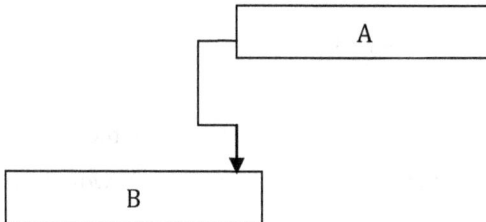

An example would of people working in shifts. The oncoming shift must start before the outgoing shift can finish.

External Dependency

A dependency may exist on a task that is external to the project. One type of external dependency could be a specific date. For example, tax returns need to be delivered to the relevant authorities by a specific date.

Alternatively, the dependency could be on an external partner beyond the ability of the organization or project team to control. For example, the project may require some particular materials or the input from a specialist (such as a legal consultant, marketing expert, insurance specialist, etc.) before the project can continue.

Tools

NETWORK DIAGRAM

A Network Diagram is a graphical representation of the dependencies between the different tasks (or work packages) which make up a project. A Network Diagram is mainly used to plan the different work packages in the project by highlighting the dependencies between them.

Network Diagrams can be used to represent a wide variety of situations. It is easiest to explain network diagrams with an example. If you have not read the previous section, *Task Dependencies*, and are not familiar with the different types of task dependencies, please quickly read through it now.

For this example we will consider a project which contains a number of tasks. These tasks are listed in the table below with their duration and their dependencies.

Task / Work Package	Expected Duration (Days)	Predecessor
Project Start	0	
A	5	Project start
B	7	A
C	10	Project start
D	3	Project start
E	9	D

F	3	B, C, E
G	6	D
H	6	Start of G + 3 days
Project End	0	F, H

These entries could be represented in a network diagram such as the one following. The network diagram includes all the tasks to be performed. It also includes the length of time expected to complete each task. To aid scheduling, the earliest and latest start and finish times for each project are listed.

Network Diagram Example

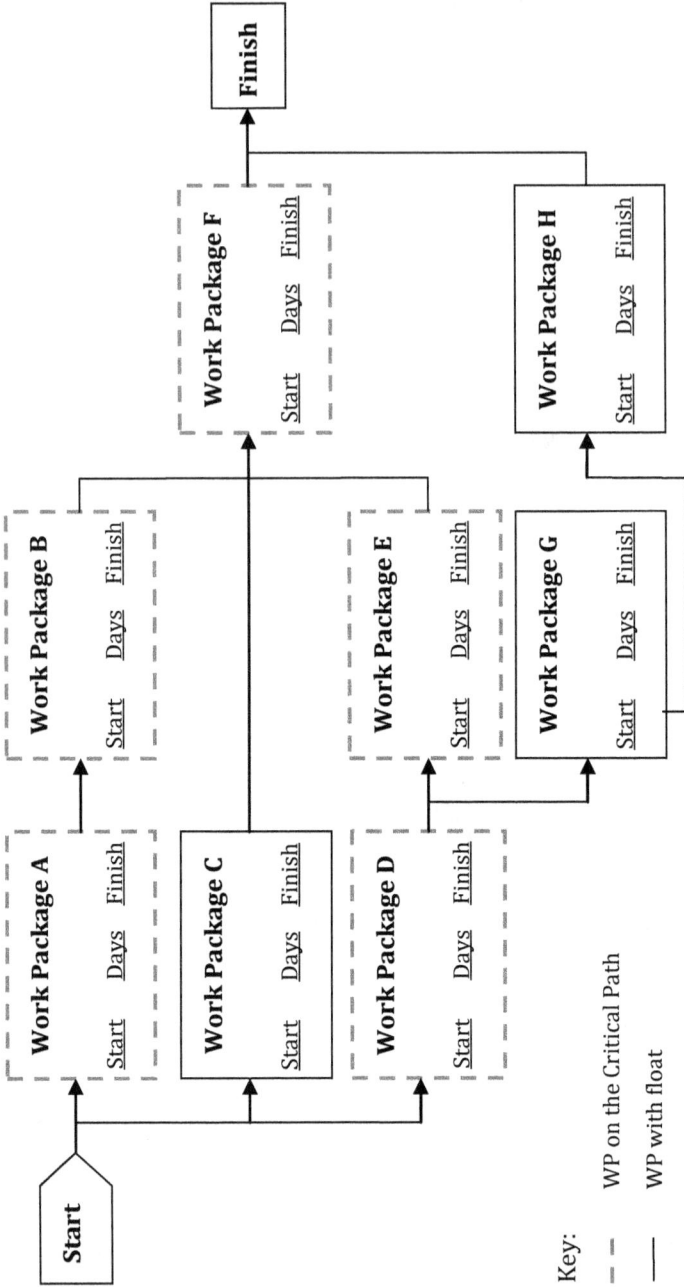

Key:

– –   WP on the Critical Path

——   WP with float

For this particular network diagram there are two critical paths: A, B, F and D, E, F. For these tasks, the earliest start date and latest start date are the same. Therefore, any delay in any of the tasks A, B, D, E, or F will cause the final project delivery date to be delayed. The work packages on the critical path have been highlighted in this example by using dashed lines to draw the boxes.

Project Critical Path

The critical path for a project defines the minimum time which is required to complete the project. Any delay to task which is on the critical path, will cause a delay to project delivery date.

The critical path of the project can be identified on a Network Diagram when the work packages have the same date for the earliest possible start date and the latest possible start date. The work packages will also have the same earliest possible finish date and latest possible finish date.

The work packages C, G, and H are not on the critical path. This can be identified in that the earliest start dates and latest start dates do not match. The difference between the earliest start date and the latest start date is referred to as the float. The float is the amount by which these tasks, which are not on the critical path, could be delayed without delaying the delivery of the completed project results.

Understanding float is important if there are insufficient resources for the whole project and one work package needs to be prioritized over another. Generally, the best work package to delay would be the work package that has the most float for the given resource. In this way, the final delivery date for the project has the best chance of being maintained while the resource shortage issue is resolved.

While most project network diagrams will include at least the information shown above, the format of a network diagram allows the option of adding additional information about each task quite easily.

Project progress through the project schedule is normally shown by putting a diagonal line through the tasks that have been started and crossing out the tasks that have been completed.

Tools

GANTT CHART

Similar to Network Diagrams, Gantt Charts are a graphical representation of a project schedule. A Gantt chart provides a visual representation of when each task will start and when it will finish. This is provided by depicting each task as a bar on a calendar. In more modern Gantt Charts, the dependencies between tasks or work packages are also shown.

Gantt Charts are not only used while planning the work package schedule, they are also helpful when communicating the status of the project. Normally, the status of the project is shown by adding a vertical line representing the current date, and the progress in each work package is shown by adding a progress bar.

This representation is visually clear and intuitive, and most people find Gantt Charts easy to use. The drawback of Gantt Charts compared to Network Diagrams is that there is only a very limited space to provide additional information about the task on the diagram.

Software tools that can be used to create Gantt charts usually include the following dependencies: independent, finish-to-start, or dependent upon a specific date. Other types of dependencies may not be possible or may be more difficult to represent.

Tools

Example of a Gantt Chart

To allow an easy comparison between a Gantt chart and a network diagram we will take the same project that was used in the network diagram example on page 300. This example project contains a number of tasks. These tasks are listed again in the table below with their duration and their dependencies.

Task / Work Package	Expected Duration (Days)	Predecessor
Project Start	0	
A	5	Project start
B	7	A
C	10	Project start
D	3	Project start
E	9	D
F	3	B, C, E
G	6	D
H	6	Start of G + 3 days
Project End	0	F, H

These entries could be represented in a Gantt chart such as the one below. The Gantt chart includes all the tasks to be performed. The length of time required to complete the task is represented by the width of the box representing

Tools

that task. The chart always shows the earliest time at which a task can be started and finished. Most software that creates Gantt Charts will highlight the critical path in a different color (typically red). Here, the critical path is shown with dotted lines.

Gantt Chart

Task	Duration	Week 5	Week 6	Week 7	Week 8
Start	0 Days				
A	5 Days				
B	7 Days				
C	10 Days				
D	3 Days				
E	9 Days				
F	3 Days				
G	6 Days				
H	6 Days				
End	0 Days				

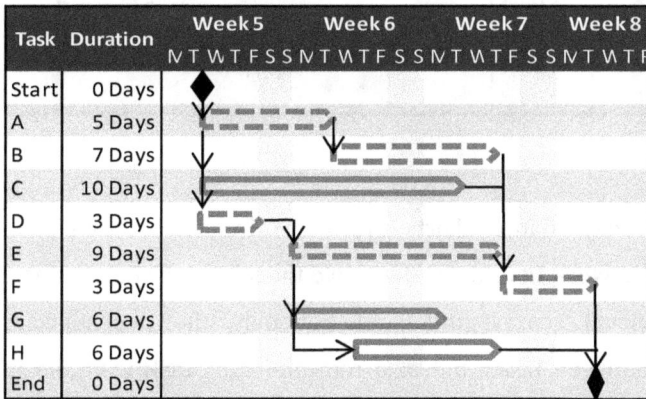

The Gantt Chart above shows the project schedule before work has started on the project.

Below is a Gantt Chart showing the same project schedule in calendar week 6. The work packages A & D have been completed, B & E are in progress, and F & H have not yet started. The thin dashed vertical line represents the current date.

Gantt Chart with Progress Bars

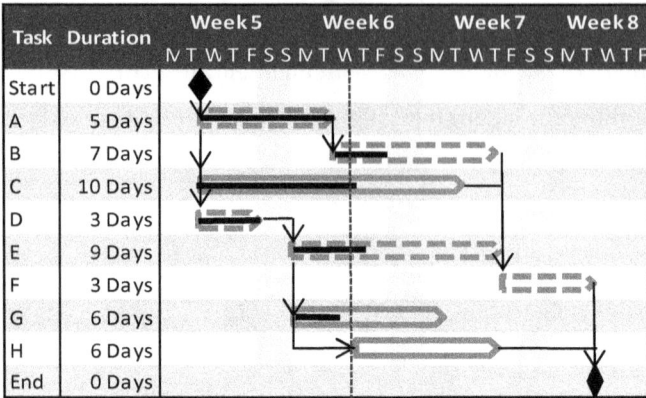

Task	Duration	Week 5 MTWTFSS	Week 6 MTWTFSS	Week 7 MTWTFSS	Week 8 MTWTF
Start	0 Days				
A	5 Days				
B	7 Days				
C	10 Days				
D	3 Days				
E	9 Days				
F	3 Days				
G	6 Days				
H	6 Days				
End	0 Days				

Today, Gantt Charts are more frequently used than Network Diagrams. They have the advantage of creating a visual representation of not only the dependencies between tasks, but also the time each task will take to complete. If the Gantt Chart has been maintained with the progress of each work package, then it is also possible to quickly identify what the overall progress of the project is.

CHAPTER 23.

RISK MANAGEMENT

In theory, risk management deals with both risks and opportunities. In practice, however, the focus is almost exclusively on managing risk. Having said that, spending at least some of the time allocated for risk management to look for and manage opportunities is worthwhile.

Risk Management Definitions:

A risk is something that, if it comes to pass, will adversely affect the project and/or the organization.

An opportunity is something that, if it comes to pass, will positively affect the project and/or the organization.

An issue is something that has actually happened or will definitely happen in the future. It will not benefit the project and / or the organization, but it is no longer avoidable and must be responded to.

An improvement is something that has actually happened, or will definitely happen in the future, that benefits the project and/or the organization.

Risk management has four basic parts:

Tools

- Identifying the risks

- Quantifying the risks

- Developing a risk mitigation strategy

- Executing and monitoring the risk mitigation strategy

Tip:

Risk management should correspond to the size and complexity of the project.

Do not spend large amounts of time examining the risks of a small and simple project unless you are using it as an exercise to develop your own or your team's skills in managing risk. The investment cost of a full and detailed analysis is likely to outweigh any benefit which could be achieved.

Obviously, this is not meant to excuse inadequate risk management for projects with significant budgets, a long implementation schedule, or major risks.

There are several different levels of risk management which could be implemented:

Tools

No risk management implemented	This is only appropriate for small projects with a short duration where the risks are understood by all major stakeholders and the risks are considered aligned with normal operational risk.
Risks identified and documented, but no explicit risk mitigation strategy is developed	This could be appropriate for small- or medium-sized projects, with a short duration, where the risks are understood by all major stakeholders and are considered to be negligible.
Major risks identified and a risk mitigation strategy documented	This may be appropriate for medium-sized projects, or a project with a small budget but longer duration.

Tools

Risks identified, quantified, risk mitigation strategy is documented, risks regularly reviewed and managed by the project manager and the project sponsor	This is the recommended approach for projects with medium or large budgets and projects with a long duration. This is also recommended for any high-risk project.

Choose the level of risk management that is appropriate to both the project and the risk tolerance level of the organization.

IDENTIFYING RISKS:

It is often quite easy to identify some of the risks to a project: key personnel may become unavailable due to illness or accident; delivery of required materials may be significantly delayed; unforeseen circumstances may cause a cash flow issue causing the project to be prematurely stopped; all the data required for the project may get destroyed inadvertently or through malicious intent.

Actually compiling a complete list of all the risks may require quite a bit of imagination. The number of different ways that things can fail or go wrong is often quite surprising! A brain storming session can be very helpful in identifying project risks. Refer to *Brainstorming* on page 262 for more details on holding a brainstorming session.

Typically, an organization has a number of operational risks that are inherent in what the organization does. It may be helpful to list the organizational risks, but there should be no need to quantify the risk or decide on a strategy for dealing with them. These risks are well understood at the executive level, and strategies for managing these risks are implemented in the normal business planning and business processes of the organization.

Tools

On top of the normal operational risks, a particular project will almost certainly have a number of risks that are specific to it. These are the risks which the project team will need to focus on while managing the project risk.

Once the risks specific to the project have been identified, add them to the project risk register.

Example of a Project Risk Register

Risk Nr.	Description	Prob. (%)	Impact (Value)	Miti- gation Strategy	Action	Due Date
R-1	Key players ill / reassigned	15%	30,000	Reduce	Define deputies	01. Aug
R-2	Supplier cannot deliver	5%	65,000	Reduce	Implement dual supplier strategy	01. Sep
R-3	Fire destroys prototype	1%	250,000	Transfer	Organize fire insurance	01. Aug
R-4	Low impact feature F-7: Development cost overrun	35%	80,000	Avoidance	Remove feature from final product	01. Mar
R-5	In case of illness or reassignment, no deputy available for specialist: Fred	5%	8,000	Accept	No action	01. Jul

Tools

Risk Nr.	Description	Prob. (%)	Impact (Value)	Miti-gation Strategy	Action	Due Date
R-6	Destruction of computer data / systems	3%	250,000	Reduce	Organize offsite backup capability	01. Aug

Tools

QUANTIFYING THE RISK:

Once a number of risks have been identified, they need to be put into some kind of perspective. Some risks are more likely to happen than others. Some risks will have negligible impact on the project, while others may have a serious impact.

Only some of these risks will be significant enough that it will be worth spending time to manage them. Other risks are either so unlikely or would have such a marginal impact that it would not be an effective use of resources to regularly manage them.

So, to quantify the risk formally, two basic pieces of information are important:

1. How likely is it that the described risk will actually happen?
2. What is the impact to the project or the organization if the described risk actually happens?

Risk Likelihood:

For each risk, make an estimate of how likely it is that the described situation will actually occur. If the organization has supporting statistics available to help, then use them. However, in most cases statistics will not be available and the estimate will be an expert's best guess.

Tools

316

Risk Impact:

Different risks will have different impacts on the project. Some will cause a delay in delivery of the project results, some will require extra funding to be injected into the project, and others may cause the project results to be worthless.

So that the risks can be evaluated, compared, and prioritized it is useful to express all the risks in monetary terms. Having done this, there are many approaches that could be used to identify which risks should be managed. Two quick and effective approaches are described below. These are the "Project Risk Diagram" and "Risk Contingency Cost".

The PMO should have created guidelines on how project risk is to be managed within the organization. If the PMO has not done this, ask the project sponsor if they have a preferred method. If not, the project manager should choose whichever approach they feel is the most appropriate.

In many organizations, the PMO provides guidelines based on fixed sums. This is useful when creating a consolidated view of risk across the complete organization for the attention of the executive management team. At an individual project level, however, it is often more useful to represent the risk volume as a percentage of the total

Tools

project budget. This provides a clearer view of the importance of the risk to the project.

Identifying Important Risks

There are many methods of identifying the most important risks to a project. Two quick and effective methods are presented below:

Approach 1: Project Risk Diagram

Project risk diagrams use a visual method to identify the most important risks to the project.

To create a project risk diagram for the project, plot the impact value against the probability of the risk occurring on a graph. See the project risk diagram below for a simple example. In general, the risks that are highly likely to occur and / or have a big impact are the risks that need to be managed.

In the project risk diagram below, the risks R1-R6 from the example of a project risk register above have been plotted. The project risk diagram shows impact against probability. The focus for the risk management would need to be placed on the risks R-3, R-4, and R-6 which have been circled. These risks have either a high impact or a high probability. This indicates that they deserve more attention than the remaining risks in the bottom left quadrant of the diagram. Any risk that landed in the top right hand quadrant of the graph would receive the highest attention from the project manager. Any high impact, high probability risk deserves the regular attention of the project manager.

Project Risk Diagram

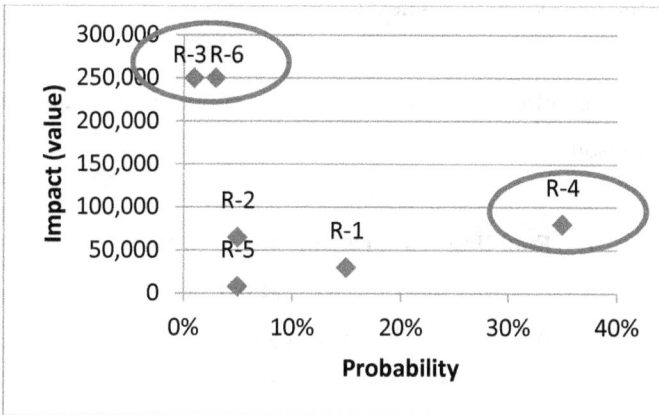

Approach 2: Risk Contingency Cost

Risk Contingency cost uses a simple calculation to identify the most important risks to the project.

Risk Contingency Costs Definitions:

Impact cost: The cost to the project / organization if the risk becomes an issue.

Contingency Cost: A sum of money which is put aside to be available in the event that a risk becomes an issue. The contingency cost is calculated as:

> Contingency Cost = Impact Cost x Probability of Occurrence

In general, the risks that are worth the most attention are the ones with the highest contingency cost.

The contingency cost method is useful for a couple of reasons.

1. **Enabling a reasonable estimate for a contingency fund to deal with the known risks**
   Adding up the contingency costs of all risks creates an estimation of the additional funding that the project is likely to need. This sum is referred to as the contingency fund.
   The organization should consider setting aside the sum of money identified by the contingency fund calculation to deal with any project issues.

2. **Enabling a comparison of the effectiveness of two different risk mitigation strategies**
   If there are two different options for mitigating a risk, then the organization will need to choose between the two possibilities. Calculating the contingency costs of each mitigation strategy will enable an objective comparison to be made. The costs of implementing the risk strategy and the

Tools

resulting contingency cost are calculated for each strategy. The strategy that results in the lowest total cost is the preferred strategy. Refer to the cost contingency calculation example later in this section for more details.

Below is an example of a completed contingency cost table.

Contingency Cost Table

Risk Nr.	Description	Prob. (%)	Impact (Value)	Contin-gency Costs	Mitigation Strategy	Action	Due Date
R-1	Key players ill / reassigned	15%	30,000	4,500	Reduce	Define deputies	01. Aug
R-2	Supplier cannot deliver	5%	65,000	3,250	Reduce	Implement dual supplier strategy	01. Sep
R-3	Fire destroys prototype	1%	250,000	2,500	Transfer	Organize fire insurance	01. Aug
R-4	Low impact feature F-7: Development cost overrun	35%	80,000	28,000	Avoidance	Remove feature from final product	01. Mar
R-5	In case of illness or reassignment, no deputy available for specialist:	5%	8,000	400	Accept	No action	01. Jul

Tools

Risk Nr.	Description	Prob. (%)	Impact (Value)	Contin-gency Costs	Mitigation Strategy	Action	Due Date
	Fred						
R-6	Destruction of computer data / systems	3%	250,000	7,500	Reduce	Organize offsite backup capability	01. Aug
	Project Contingency fund			46,150			

Notes on the contingency Cost Table:

The probability of a risk occurring is always less than 100% (100% would mean that it would definitely happen, therefore it is no longer a risk, it is an issue). Therefore, when the impact cost is multiplied with the probability to create the contingency cost, the contingency cost is smaller than the impact cost.

It is highly unlikely that all risks will become issues, so funding does not need to be available to cover the full impact cost of every risk.

The opportunities that the project team identified during project planning can be included into the contingency risk calculation in the same way. Similar to risks, some opportunities may bare fruit while others may not. The benefits to the project from the identified opportunities may help to counter the contingency costs of the risks. This will reduce the size of the contingency fund that would be advised for the project.

If using a contingency fund, ensure that it is understood that the contingency cost for each individual risk is not the actual amount that is at risk in each case. Collected together over all the risks, the contingency sum is normally a good guide to the overall project risk. However, for specific risks, it may not be sufficient. For example, in the table above, if risk R-2 occurs, then it will cost the project an unplanned 65,000. The total risk contingency is however only 46,150. However, if instead risk R-5 is the only risk which occurs during project execution, then the project will only have an unplanned cost of 8,000.

When evaluating the contingency fund, remember that the probability estimate most likely originated from someone's best guess. Therefore, treat the figures as a guide and not as an exact truth.

The following example shows how two different risk mitigation strategies can be compared to the base risk (doing nothing) using a contingency risk calculation. This type of calculation enables a more informed decision to be made when choosing between different risk mitigation strategies.

Tools

Risk Contingency Calculation Example:

A travel company takes bookings all year round, but receives the highest bookings request rates between the 1st of January and the 31st of March.

It is October and the current IT systems are at 78% of the available processing capacity. The capacity planning team has modeled the load. They state that there exists a 60% chance that the existing IT systems will fail for at least 5 hours each month in January, February, and March due to overload.

Based on past experience, the management of the travel company have identified that the direct costs of not being able accept bookings for over 15 minutes is 40.000 per hour due to lost business. The indirect costs from loss of reputation are considered negligible unless the IT systems are offline for over 1 day – which the capacity planning team has stated is highly unlikely to be caused through overload.

The travel company's IT supplier is willing to make extra computing capacity available for three months at a cost of 190.000. The capacity planning team's models show that this would reduce the chance of a system overload to 5% or less.

The capacity planning team has also suggested that an

application expert be brought in to review the IT systems. The capacity planning team is not able to predict the exact benefit here. However, they expect that by implementing the measures recommended by the expert, the chance of a system overload will be reduced to 15% or less. The cost of the application expert and implementing the changes are estimated to be 80,000.

Which option should the organization follow?

Calculate the baseline:

First of all, calculate the cost of continuing as now:

The cost of each computer failure would be 5*40,000 = 200,000

The chance of a computer outage each month is 60%.

$$200,000\left(\frac{60}{100}\right) + 200,000\left(\frac{60}{100}\right) + 200,000\left(\frac{60}{100}\right)$$

$$= 120,000 + 120,000 + 120,000$$

$$= 360,000$$

Therefore, the expected cost of doing nothing is 360.000.

Calculate the cost of purchasing the extra computer capacity:

The cost of a computer outage remains the same: 200,000.

The chance of an outage each month reduces to 5%.

The investment cost is 200,000:

$$190{,}000 + 200{,}000\left(\frac{5}{100}\right) + 200{,}000\left(\frac{5}{100}\right) + 200{,}000\left(\frac{5}{100}\right)$$

$$= 190{,}000 + 10{,}000 + 10{,}000 + 10{,}000$$

$$= 220{,}000$$

Therefore, the total cost of purchasing the additional computing capacity is 230,000.

Calculate the cost of the application expert:

The cost of a computer outage remains the same: 200,000. The chance of an outage each month reduces to 15%. The investment cost is 80,000:

$$80{,}000 + 200{,}000\left(\frac{15}{100}\right) + 200{,}000\left(\frac{15}{100}\right) + 200{,}000\left(\frac{15}{100}\right)$$

$$= 80{,}000 + 30{,}000 + 30{,}000 + 30{,}000$$

$$= 170{,}000$$

Based on these risk calculations, management would be advised to purchase the support of the application expert and implement their advice before the peak period begins.

Tools

Even though risk contingency cost does not allow for all circumstances, it is a useful tool to put the risks to a project into perspective.

RISK MITIGATION STRATEGIES

The purpose of developing risk mitigation strategies is to reduce the level of risk to the project or the organization. While developing these strategies, keep in mind that the risk mitigation strategy must be appropriate to the actual risk. In particular, it is not advisable to spend more to avoid a risk than the cost to the organization would be if the risk became an issue.

For each of the identified risks, a risk strategy will need to be implemented which will cover at least one of the following:

- Eliminate the risk to the project completely
- Reduce the chance of the risk occurring
- Reduce the impact to the project should the risk become an issue
- Create a contingency plan for the event that the risk becomes an issue

General risk mitigation strategies include:

Acceptance: The risk is documented and agreed to be an acceptable risk by the project sponsor.

Avoidance: The applicable part of the project (e.g. work package, deliverable) is removed

Tools

from the scope of the project in agreement with the project sponsor.

Reduction: Steps are taken to reduce the chance of the risk occurring, or the impact the risk would have, or both.

An example could be: avoiding a cheaper supplier with unknown delivery capability and instead using a more expensive supplier who is known to be reliable.

Regular communication to create awareness and regular monitoring of major risks are often key factors in reducing the probability of a risk becoming an issue.

Transference: Make a third party responsible for the risk. This can be done by purchasing insurance or by outsourcing the work to a third party who is more capable of performing the necessary work than the organization itself is.

Particularly if transference is the chosen strategy, be aware of what is actually being achieved. If a highly risky piece of work is passed to a third party, does the risk go away? Normally, the answer is no: The risk has been changed (and hopefully reduced) to one of late delivery or non-delivery by the firm who has won the contract.

The purchase of insurance is similar. For example, the purchase of fire insurance will not stop a fire occurring, or stop the fire from destroying property, equipment or knowledge. Insurance will simply provide funds for the organization to create replacements. A more useful risk mitigation strategy may be to review the working environment to reduce the potential of the fire occurring and installing fire alarms to reduce the impact of a fire if one occurs.

Tools

MANAGING RISK DURING PROJECT EXECUTION:

As the project progresses, the risks will change. Some risks will disappear because they can no longer occur. The project team may also discover alternative, improved methods of further reducing the project risk for specific known risks. Finally, additional risks may be discovered as the project team learns more about the project.

Particularly for longer or riskier projects, the risk register should be reviewed on a regular basis to ensure that it reflects the current situation.

- Any new risks need to be added.
- Any risks which can no longer occur need to be removed.
- The strategy for each risk should be quickly reviewed to ensure that the strategy is still appropriate.
- If the PMO is tracking the total project risk for the organization, then feedback needs to be made to the PMO regarding the updated risk situation.

Tools

CHAPTER 24.

PEOPLE MANAGEMENT

As with any management position, it is an important part of the project manager's role to manage the people working in the project team. The tools that are introduced on the following pages are useful aids to managing staff in a project environment.

Tools

TYPES OF AUTHORITY AND POWER

To manage people effectively, it helps to have an understanding of the different types of authority and power that exist within an organization. There are two broad sources of authority: Positional and personal.

Positional authority is, in essence, the authority transferred to a person by an organization to enable them to perform a particular function. They are given the ability to control budgets and other resources within the organization. A line manager is typically given the ability to motivate their staff by rewarding them financially or assigning them to work which is particularly interesting. They also have disciplinary authority over their staff.

Personal authority, on the other hand, is not directly bestowed on the person by the organization, but is developed by the person themselves. Sources of personal authority are: having a particular knowledge or expertise required by the organization, being a charismatic person who is able to lead and inspire others, having a strong personal network, and being better informed than others.

Within a project, these authorities are typically distributed as follows:

The project sponsor has positional authority. They have control of the budget and the other resources that are required to complete the project. Ideally, they will also have personal authority from their experience, knowledge and leadership skills.

The project manager has a limited amount of positional authority. This derives from the project sponsor for the term of the project only. A project manager needs to develop personal authority. This can come from expert knowledge of project management, networking skills, personal charisma, or just being able to motivate others to get things done.

All the members of the project team will have strong personal authority. This is because they will have expert skills and may also control resources that are essential to complete the project successfully. This was the reason why they were included in the project team.

TEAM BUILDING

The most important ingredient to running a successful project is to have a capable, motivated team working towards a common goal. For our purposes, team building is about taking a group of individuals from different parts of the organization, and getting them to work together as a team to create the required project results.

As initially proposed by Bruce Tuckman (and later expanded on with Mary Ann Jensen), most project teams will go through the following organizational development phases: Forming, Storming, Norming, Performing, and Adjourning. Understanding and supporting this process can help a project team get to the productive "Performing" phase as quickly as possible.

Project Team Performance Over Time

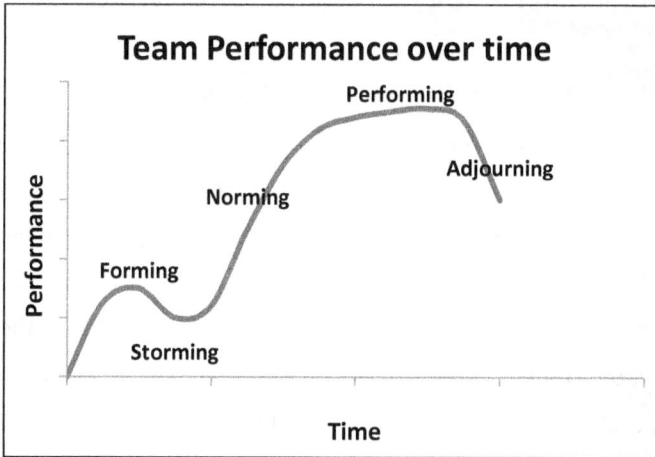

Team Performance over time

Performing

Adjourning

Norming

Forming

Storming

Performance

Time

Tools

Forming:

In the initial phase of team building, forming, the team organizes itself into a certain structure. Serious issues and feelings are not discussed during this phase. The team members typically focus on understanding the project goal. They will be gathering their own impressions of the work to be completed, the achievability of the project goal, and their colleagues.

Assuming that the project tasks and goals are reasonable then this is normally a comfortable phase of project team development. Enthusiasm and confidence are high.

Storming:

As the team members grow to trust one another and the project organization, the team members will begin to challenge the status quo. They will also start to challenge each other's opinions or question the project's approach.

Some team members may find this phase stressful and unpleasant. This is particularly true if they are not used to having their expertise challenged. Indeed, in terms of getting project tasks done, this is not a very productive time. However, if an atmosphere of tolerance for the opinions of others is created, then this is often one of the most creative phases of the project team development. By challenging the status quo, new ideas and ways of working can be discussed. These ideas, suggestions, and improvements have the potential to drive the project team

Tools

forward and improve performance over the rest of the project lifecycle.

If this phase is managed badly, with little tolerance for the ideas and opinions of others, interpersonal issues can be introduced into the project team, which are very difficult to overcome in a later phase.

Norming:

Everyone will have found their place and role in the team. Some of the ideas proposed during the storming phase will have dropped by the wayside and some will have been implemented. The team members will have accepted the current way of working and their role in the team as a fact of life. The project team is now concentrated on achieving common goals. Productivity improves considerably during this phase.

Performing:

Particularly for longer running projects with project team members committed full time to the project, the team may reach the performing phase.

In the performing phase, project teams are highly motivated and effective. The team members will work together to find the most effective method of achieving the project goals.

Tools

The project manager will let the project team make most of the decisions themselves during this phase, stepping in only if the project is starting to stray off track. The main function of the project manager during this phase is to ensure that the project team is given the space and resources to perform, and as little outside interference as possible.

Adjourning:

Adjourning is the process of breaking up the project team once the project has completed.

In project where each team member has only committed a few hours a week there may be a feeling of accomplishment – a task well done.

In projects where the project team has worked closely and intensely together for a longer period of time, some of the team members may feel insecure about moving out of the project and into a new role. To help alleviate insecurity, it is helpful to make sure that the line manager of each team member talks to their staff regarding how they will be integrated back into the normal line work. There may also be a sense of loss as the team splits ups. If this is likely, it is helpful to the team to have a project closing event (after the Lessons Learned session is often a good time for it) to give the team members a chance to say goodbye to each other as they move on to other work.

Tools

SKILL MANAGEMENT

Projects are the perfect environment for people within the organization to develop new skills. In a large number of projects, a secondary goal of the project is skill development. Skill development could be in focus for any member(s) of the project team, including the project manager.

Including skill development as formal goal of the project has a number of benefits:

- The skill development can be formally assessed and recorded. This development and assessment can be included as part of the regular performance and development review which the organization has
- The project budget and plan can be expanded to make allowances for the extra time and costs to cover training, coaching, and other forms of support required to support the development process
- It is a motivating factor for the team member
- It helps the organization to keep better track of the skills which have been developed within the organization

Hard Skills:

Hard skills reflect the technical skills required to perform a particular job. These skills almost always improve in a project, as the project team develops solutions to the project challenges. These are, however, rarely captured and recorded. This means that many organizations find it difficult to identify which skills they have available. Even if these skills are captured and recorded, then they are often only captured as an entry in the personnel file for the employee. This means the information is only available if someone looks directly in the personnel file for a particular person.

In general, a skills database containing all the skills which are known to have been developed within the organization, including a reference to which people have those skills, is more useful than maintaining the information in the personnel files. It is unlikely that someone would search the personnel files of everyone in the organization to find someone with a particular skill. If a database of skills is available, it is far easier to search this. Remember that when people move to different functional areas within an organization, their skill record is often forgotten by all but the people working most closely together with them.

Tools

340

Soft Skills:

Soft skills are the non-technical skills that enable a person to be more productive when working together with others. They include:

- Communication skills
- Leadership skills
- Ability to resolve conflicts
- Ability to motivate others
- Self confidence
- Empathy
- Ability to work in a team
- Ability to pass on their knowledge and skills to others

These kinds of skills often require coaching and experience to develop rather than just a textbook education.

Tools

COMMUNICATION

In this section, we will discuss the Source, Message, Chanel, and Receiver (SMCR) model of communication. The purpose of discussing the SMCR model here is to provide an aid in understanding what actually happens when people communicate with each other. Understanding how communication works helps to identify where communication difficulties could or do occur.

> **Communication**
> Communication is the process by which we share information with others using a common system of signs, signals, or behaviors.

In a project, there is a high demand for information to be shared efficiently and effectively. A few examples are:

- The project requestor will need to make sure that their requirements have been understood
- The project manager will need to gather the status from the team members and use it to inform the project sponsor and other stakeholders of the project status

- The team members will need to understand the status of prerequisite tasks so that they know when to start their own tasks
- Any issues will need to be communicated clearly and rapidly to the person who can solve them

Effective communication (the efficient and effective sharing of information) is an essential part of successful project management. Most project managers spend about 70% of their time communicating. Although the project team usually spends more time on tasks than on communicating, it is still an important success factor that they are able to share their expertise with the other team members and, if necessary, raise issues quickly, clearly, and concisely.

The SMCR Model

David Berlo expanded on Claude Shannon and Warren Weaver's first model of communication to create the SMCR model. Previous communication models had focused mainly on the technical method of encoding and decoding information so that it can be transmitted from one place to another. Instead, the SMCR model focuses on the message that a person wants to send and the reception of the message, by the person for whom it is intended. It is this focus on the message and the people involved that is useful to us here.

Tools

The SMCR Model includes:

Source   A person with something to communicate.

              The Source's ability to send their message
              depends on many factors, including:

              • The person's communication skills
              • Their attitude towards both the
                audience and themselves
              • Their knowledge of the subject at
                hand
              • The social system in place (this
                includes culture, values, beliefs,
                religion, society at large)

              The Source encodes the message into a
              format for transmission. In our case,
              possible formats for transmission include
              body language, tonal inflection, written
              word, pictures, or other visual aids.

Message   The Message is what the Source sends.

              This includes:

              • The content: The message which
                the Source is sending

- Elements: Include things such as gestures and other body language which add additional meaning to the content
- Treatment: Refers to how the message is packaged for delivery. Too much packaging and the message may get lost. Too little packaging and the receiver may not be able to put the message into context or may not consider the message to be culturally acceptable
- Structure: Describes how the message is organized. It could be considered to be the framework of the content.
  In general, a well-structured message is easier to interpret than the same content delivered in a random order
- Code: The form of the message (speech, written text)

Channel	This refers to which of the five senses will be used by the receiver to receive the message.

In a business environment, this is generally

Tools

restricted to hearing and seeing.

Receiver   The Receiver is the person for whom the message is intended.

The Receivers' ability to understand the message being sent is dependent upon their:

- Communication skills
- Attitude towards both the Source and the message. This includes a personal interest in actually receiving the message being sent and the Receiver's personal evaluation regarding whether or not the Source is worth paying attention to
- Level of knowledge of the subject at hand
- Social system in place (this includes culture, values, beliefs, religion, society at large)

The Receiver decodes the Message sent by the Source and (hopefully) attempts to understand it

Tools

So how does this help us to communicate effectively in a project environment?

In the SMCR model, it becomes clear that the most effective communication occurs when:

- The Source and the Receiver(s) are as similar as possible. This means that they have the same culture, technical knowledge, expectations of appropriate packaging, etc.
- The message is sent in a way that the Receiver can understand the content
- The Receiver believes that the Source is someone worth listening to
- The Source believes that the Receiver is someone worth talking to

As an example: Two lawyers (operating in the same legal system) will package a Message in a particular way. The Message will be clearly understood by both of them. To a person outside of the legal profession, the Message may be unclear or even completely unintelligible.

In a project environment, almost all the requirements for good communication have been removed. The team members have been brought together precisely because they come from different backgrounds, have different areas of expertise, etc. It is not unrealistic for a project

Tools

team to include a Project Manager, a Legal Advisor, a Salesman, an Engineer, and an Accountant.

- Each of these team members has very different "cultural" backgrounds
- They each use a separate language specific to their daily work
- They will each package a message differently in their daily work

It is very likely that when they talk to each other, they will have communication difficulties.

It is then essential for effective communication that each Source is very aware of:

- Who they are talking to
- Differences in the level of knowledge between themselves and the Receiver(s) with respect to the subject being discussed
- The "cultural diversity" between the different team members
- The right amount of "packaging". Enough to make sure that people pay attention to the message, but not so much that the message is obscured

In particular, the project manager needs to be highly aware of the potential for communication issues and facilitate as necessary to improve communication within the project team.

Tools

CHAPTER 25.

COST MANAGEMENT

As with any managerial role, project management requires that the project manager make the most effective use of the available resources. One of the most important resources available to the project will be the project budget. This budget may be expressed in terms of hours of work, a fixed monetary sum, or some other method relevant to the organization.

Any project has costs associated with it. Depending upon the project, the costs may include:

- Investments costs
- Materials
- Time (in the form of salary, rent, and other similar costs)
- Machine usage
- Organizational costs (management costs, rent, ...)

If project costs are poorly managed, it is very easy to end up in a situation where the available budget has been spent, but the project has not been completed. The project manager is then put in the position of requiring a budget extension from the project sponsor, but cannot explain why the original budget was insufficient.

Tools

By managing the costs throughout the project, the project manager has the opportunity to respond quickly should the project start to exceed the planned budget. The project manager then has the opportunity to make changes to control the costs before they get out of hand. Even if the project manager is unable to correct the situation, they can bring the situation to the attention of the project sponsor. This lets the project sponsor make an early decision on which steps would be necessary to control costs, expand the budget, or to stop the project. This reduces the risk to the organization.

This chapter introduces two cost management tools. Earned Value Management (EVM) and the Burndown Chart. EVM is a powerful tool; even the simplified version presented here is capable of managing large and complex projects. It is particularly valuable when large pieces of the project work will be contracted out to third parties. For smaller and financially less complicated projects, the Burndown Chart will probably be the better choice.

Tools

SIMPLIFIED EARNED VALUE MANAGEMENT (EVM)

Earned Value Management is an excellent method of tracking costs against progress. It is a very useful tool in helping to show if a project is being delivered on time and within budget.

There are a number of variations of EVM which can become quite complex - there are entire books written on the subject! The simplified version presented here will be fine for most projects and will provide an introduction for anyone looking to learn more about EVM.

EVM is particularly valuable when deliverables or multiple work packages will be given to third parties to complete. The third party is then paid for each completed work package according to the originally agreed value, rather than using a time and materials method of billing. This enables the project manager to manage the costs of the third party reliably.

Introduction:

Early in a project, the work to be performed is split into clearly defined work packages. Each work package has a cost associated with it. Since project costs are a mixture of hours, materials, and other costs, it is usually simplest to put all of them into monetary terms. However, the method works equally well when just tracking project hours.

Tools

Earned Value Management (EVM) Definitions:

Planned Value (PV) is the budgeted cost of the planned work. In other words, PV is the value that the project plan states is budgeted for the work package or project.

Earned Value (EV) is the value that the project has created so far. This is calculated as the sum of the planned values for each completed work package.

Actual Cost (AC) is the amount actually spent so far.

In this simplified version, the assumption is made that there is no value created by a work package until the work package has been completed. Many variations exist where there is a certain value created when a work package is started. For instance, the materials required to start the work package have an intrinsic value that could be recovered even if the work package was not completed. The remaining value is acquired when the work package is finished.

Returning to our simplified version of EVM, as each work package completes, the project acquires the value that the project plan stated that the work package would cost to complete. The project does not obtain the value that the work actually cost to complete.

Tools

> **Note:**
> In all the examples discussed on the following pages, the assumption is made that there was no significant planning error.

Here is an example of a simple project schedule with 10 work packages in three work streams. To keep the example simple, each work package has one person working full time on it.

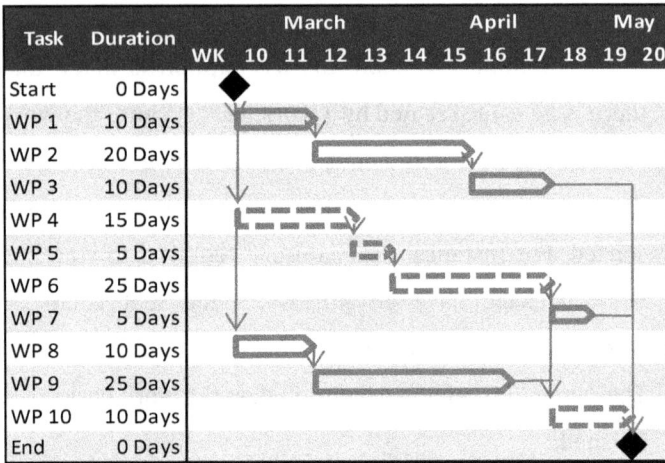

Task	Duration	March WK 10	11	12	13	April 14	15	16	17	18	May 19	20
Start	0 Days											
WP 1	10 Days											
WP 2	20 Days											
WP 3	10 Days											
WP 4	15 Days											
WP 5	5 Days											
WP 6	25 Days											
WP 7	5 Days											
WP 8	10 Days											
WP 9	25 Days											
WP 10	10 Days											
End	0 Days											

To put this into monetary terms, we will assume that each day's effort (including rent, materials, and all other costs) costs 1.000,-. Therefore, the Planned Value (PV) of the project is 135.000,-. (See table below.)

Work Package	Planned Value (PV)
Work Package 1	10,000
Work Package 2	20,000
Work Package 3	10,000
Work Package 4	15,000
Work Package 5	5,000
Work Package 6	25,000
Work Package 7	5,000
Work Package 8	10,000
Work Package 9	25,000
Work Package 10	10,000
Total	*135,000*

If we combine the information regarding the planned value of the work package with the information in the project schedule, then we will be able to see which packages will have been completed by which date. Since the value of each package is known, we know which value the project should have achieved at any date during the project lifecycle.

The Planned Value of the project can be plotted quite simply on a graph (Planned Value against time). By comparing the Planned Value for the project against the Earned Value it is possible to see how the project is progressing. See the examples below:

Tools

EVM: Normal Project Achievement

For example, let us pretend that we are in week 8 of the project, and the work packages 1, 2, 3, 4, 5, 8, & 9 have been completed. Work package 6 is approximately 50% complete.

The project schedule would show the status like this:

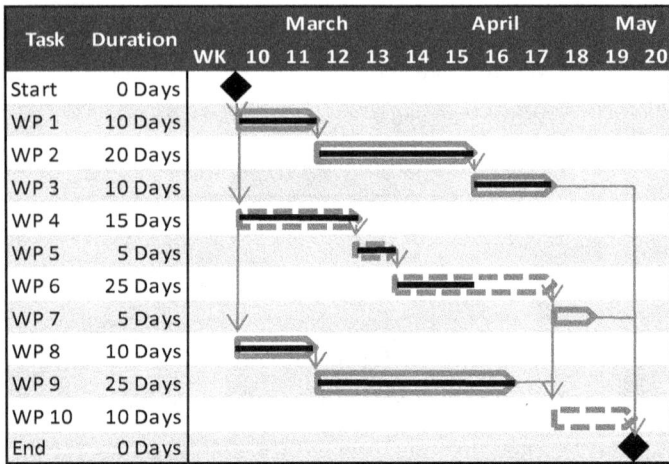

And the earned value table will look like this:

Work Package	Planned Value (PV)	Earned Value (EV)
Work Package 1	10,000	10,000
Work Package 2	20,000	20,000
Work Package 3	10,000	10,000
Work Package 4	15,000	15,000

Work Package 5	5,000	5,000
Work Package 6	25,000	
Work Package 7	5,000	
Work Package 8	10,000	10,000
Work Package 9	25,000	25,000
Work Package 10	10,000	
Total	*135,000*	*95.000*

In other words, the value of the delivered results in this example is currently 95,000.-. This is represented on the graph below that shows the planned value and the earned value over the first 8 weeks of the project:

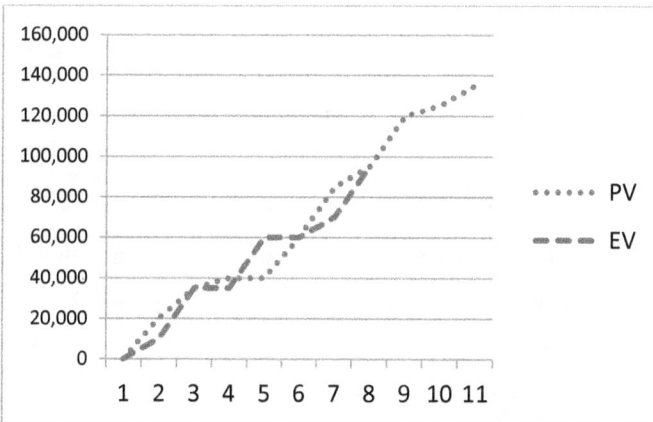

This graph shows a fairly normal project progress. The earned value (dashed line), as measured by the completed work packages, closely follows the planned value (dotted line).

Tools

357

In this simplified version of Earned Value Management (EVM), we have not created any value until a work package is completed. Therefore, work package 6 has not yet created any value for the project even though it is 50% complete. This is a reasonable assumption in a service industry project (software development, legal advice, etc.) where an incomplete work package or deliverable has little intrinsic value. In different industries, for example construction, it may be appropriate to assign a value to every work package started. This is because even if the task were not to be completed by the person who is assigned to do it, the materials that have been paid for can still be recovered. Therefore, there is some value to the organization or customer from the work package even though it is not yet complete.

EVM: Normal Project Achievement with Actual Costs Added

Obviously, not just the value earned is of interest. It is also important to know how much it cost to earn that value. To identify this we just add another line to our graph showing the actual cost accumulated over the period of the project. In this particular case, we have a linear cost line. This would be typical for a dedicated project team where most of the costs are directly related to the hours worked.

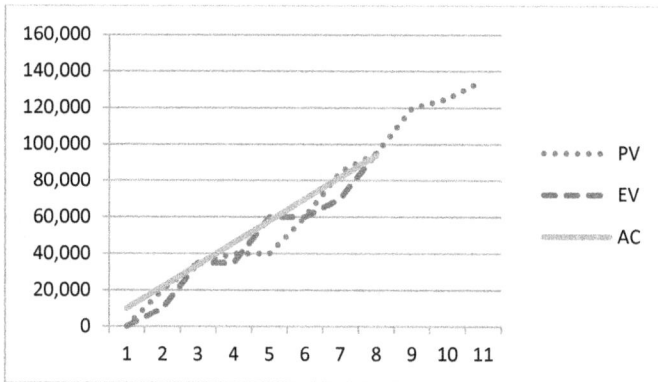

This graph is a repeat of the one above with the actual costs added. As shown previously, the earned value (dashed line) closely follows the planned value (dotted line), which means that the project schedule is under control. Adding the line showing the actual costs (full line) to the graph demonstrates that the costs are also following the planned expenditure. This project is performing according to plan and shows no cause for concern.

EVM: Poor Project Performance

This graph below shows a project that is underperforming. The earned value (dashed line), as measured by completed work packages, is not keeping up with the planned value (dotted line). But, the actual cost (full line) is closely following the planned value (dotted line). If nothing happens to change this trend, then this project can be expected to require a considerable additional investment of time and resources before the desired results are created.

Tools

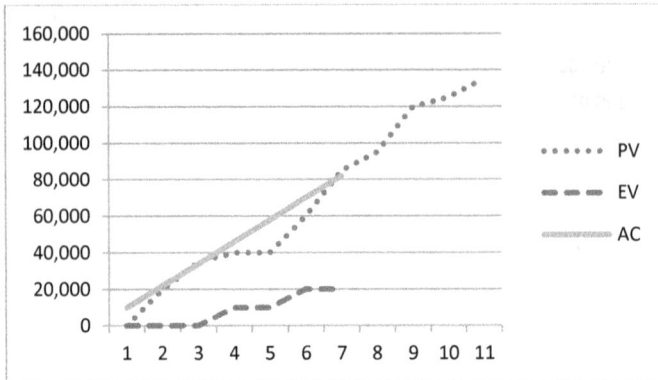

This project needs to be investigated to discover what has gone wrong. The project sponsor may decide to stop the project early to avoid wasting further resources on this struggling project.

EVM: Project with Insufficient Resources Committed

The graph below shows a project is not using the resources at the planned rate. It is most likely under resourced. The project is unlikely to complete on schedule because the earned value (dashed line) is not keeping track with the planned value (dotted line).

However, the actual costs (full line) spent on the project are following the earned value (dashed line) quite closely. This means that the actual expenditure is closely matched to the planned costs for the work which has been completed. Therefore, the reason the project will not achieve the planned schedule is because there are insufficient resources committed to the project.

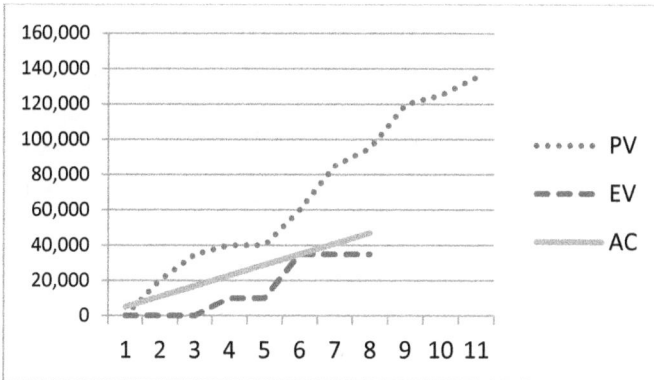

This project needs to be investigated to identify why the planned resources are not being committed. If the project manager does not have sufficient gravitas to ensure that the necessary resources are committed as originally planned, then the project sponsor needs to become involved. The project sponsor has the options of accepting the delay in project delivery, ensuring extra resources are committed to the project to bring it back onto schedule, or cutting the project early because the required resources are not available to complete the project on time.

EVM: Project Over-Performing with Respect to Costs

The graph below shows a project that is delivering results on time. However, the actual costs (full line) are less than the planned value (dotted line). It is likely that the project is slightly under-resourced. Despite this, the project is completing the work packages on schedule.

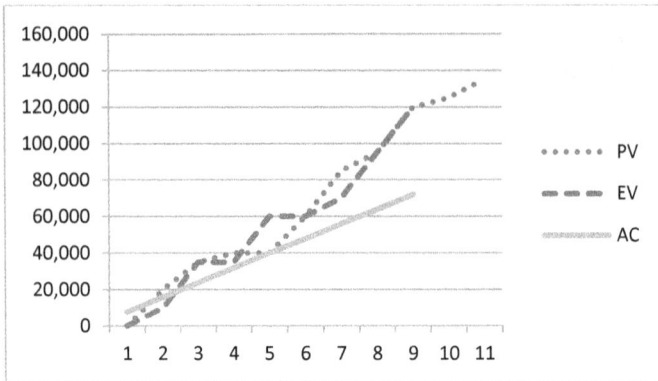

Assuming the quality delivered is in line with expectations, this is a very good result.

EVM: Project Over-Performing with Respect to the Delivery Schedule

The graph below shows a project that is being completed faster than expected. This project has costs that far exceed the planned value. This might be a cause of considerable concern. However, the graph also shows that the work packages are being completed in line with the planned expenditure value. Therefore, this graph is showing that resources are overcommitted to this project.

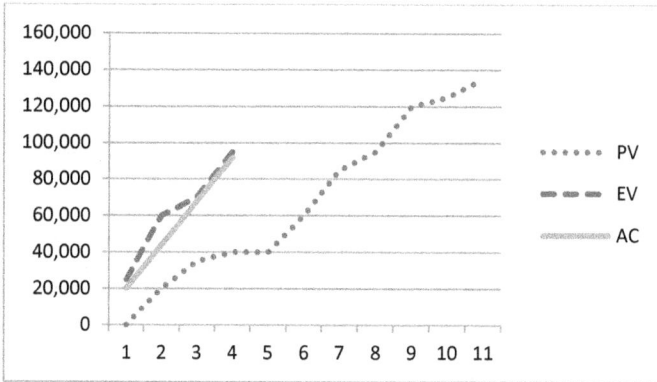

This project will most likely complete before schedule but costs will be in line with the original plan. Again, this is an indication of a good result.

Tools

BURNDOWN CHART

A simpler alternative to EVM for managing costs is a Burndown Chart.

A Burndown Chart is a simple graph that plots the value of the outstanding tasks against the duration of the project. The baseline for the burndown chart is simply a straight line between the starting point (day 0, value of all work packages) and the project completion date (final day, no open tasks so the remaining value to be created is zero).

This type of cost control mechanism is particularly useful for projects where the main cost is due to labor and not materials. Significant, irregular investment in materials costs will mean that the project costs are often a long way from the expected linear cost line. This may cause undue concern regarding the progress of the project and adjustments would need to be made to the baseline to reflect this.

Because this type of cost control graph is mainly used in an environment where the main costs are labor-related, burndown charts often show estimated hours remaining to complete the open work packages against project duration, rather than a monetary figure. Refer to the example below:

Tools

Project Burndown Chart

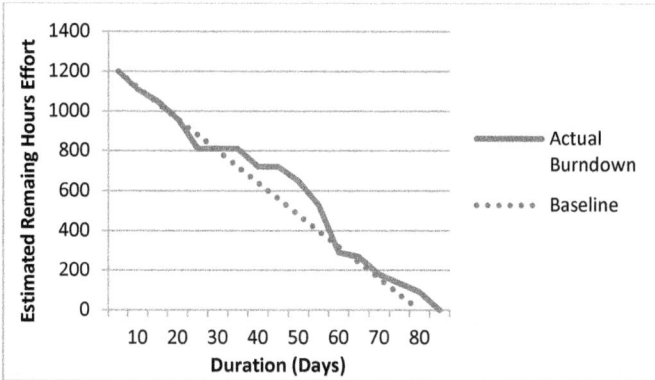

This burndown chart shows a reasonably well managed project with a slight schedule overrun. The actual burndown (full line) closely follows the expected baseline (dotted line).

CHAPTER 26.

TIME MANAGEMENT

Making the best use of your time is a key success factor in any business environment. Project Management is no exception.

There are many books and courses available on how to optimize the use of your time. If you have not been introduced to time management techniques in the past, then a good book or course on time management it is definitely worth the investment.

Here is a simple, yet very effective, starting point for optimizing the use of your time:

In the evening, before you go home:

Take a piece of paper and list all the things you need to do. Split work which will take longer than 1-2 days to complete into smaller tasks.

In the margin on the left, add a priority (A, B, C). You should not have more than three priority "A" tasks. If you do, you are either overloaded with work (so find someone to help reduce your workload), or you need to review your prioritization.

You should have something similar to the table below:

X	B	Boring task that needs to be done by next week
	C	Interesting task due next month
		Big job
	B	Big job, task 1
	A	Big job, task 2
	B	Big Job, task 3
	A	Important task
	C	Need to do sometime task
	(A)	Your boss has requested that this task be completed as soon as possible

If the task is very urgent, put a ring around the priority to remind you that it is urgent.

Draw a line at the bottom of your list.

When you start work the next day, review your list. <u>Start work with your priority A tasks first</u>. If you get the important tasks for that day done, then you will have had a successful day. So get started on those tasks before you start on anything else. Later in the day, you can pick up the next most important remaining tasks and work on those.

Tools

As the day goes on, put a cross in the margin for any tasks which have been completed. Add any new tasks to the bottom of your list.

As the day progresses, your sheet of paper should look something like this:

X	B	Boring task that needs to be done by next week
	C	Interesting Task due next month
		Big Job 1
	B	Big Job 1, Task 1
X	A	Big Job 1, Task 2
	B	Big Job 1, Task 3
X	A	Important task
	C	Need to do sometime task
X	(A)	Your boss has requested that this task be completed as soon as possible
	B	Call supplier to discuss
	B	Call supplier to discuss ...
	A	Prepare for big meeting on ...
	C	Extra task of little importance

At the end of the day, review your progress.

- Did you get all your top priority tasks completed? If yes, then congratulate yourself. You have had a successful day

- Are new tasks being added faster than you can complete them?

  Note: work tends to come in batches, so you might need to review this over a period of time.

- Are there any low priority tasks that have been on your list for a long time?

  If yes, do they really need to be done?

  If yes, ask yourself if they could be taken off your list and assigned to someone else.

- Create a new list for tomorrow.

It is important to create your new list in the evening before you leave for home and not in the morning before you start work. In the evening, all the tasks are still fresh in your mind. In the morning, it is easy to become distracted by a need to be "doing something", instead of planning and prioritizing your work for the day. Knowing that all the tasks for tomorrow are safely written down helps many people to stop thinking about those tasks and they find it easier to relax properly.

This is a very simple time management tool – but it is surprisingly effective. Try it for a month and see if it helps you.

Tools

Tools

Appendix

This Appendix shows some sample templates to be used in Stripped Down Project Management. The purpose of these documents is twofold:

1. They are here to save you the time and effort of developing similar documents yourself
2. They provide a reference for the documents referred to in this book.

These templates have proven themselves in a large number of projects. If your organization does not yet have standardized project document templates, then please feel free to use these as a starting point.

WORK PACKAGE TEMPLATE

Project name:			
Project manager:		**Project Number:**	
WP Name:			
WP Number:			
WP Responsible:			
Prerequisite WP:		**Dependent WP:**	
Planned start:	YYYY-MM-DD	**Planned End:**	YYYY-MM-DD
Version:	V0.1	**Amended on:**	YYYY-MM-DD

Brief description of the Work Package
<Short description of the work package>

Work Package Deliverables
<List the main deliverables of the work package>

Work Package Schedule	
Work Package Start:	YYYY-MM-DD
Milestone	**Due Date**
<Milestone 1>	YYYY-MM-DD
<Milestone 2>	
<...>	
Work Package End:	YYYY-MM-DD

Resource Planning				
Required Resources	**Planned Start**	**Planned End**	**Available hours per week**	**Total Available hours**

COMMUNICATION PLAN TEMPLATE

Stakeholder	Role	Type of communication	Frequency
<Project Sponsor>	Project Sponsor	Steering Board Meeting	Monthly
<Steering Board>	Steering Board	Steering Board Meeting	Monthly
<Project Team>		Project team meeting	Weekly
<... any other required contacts...>		<eMail / Letter / Telephone / ...>	
<Anyone who needs to know the status of the project>		<eMail / Newsletter / ...>	

SCOPE STATEMENT TEMPLATE

Project Name:			
Project Manager:		Project Number:	
Project Sponsor:			
Type of project:			
Project Start:	YYYY-MM-DD	Project end:	YYYY-MM-DD
Version:	V0.1	Amended on:	YYYY-MM-DD

Brief description of the project

<List the main goals (external view) of the project>

Project Deliverables

<List the main deliverables (internal view) of the project>

<List the deliverables which mark the major milestones in the project>

Detailed Project Scope

Requirements Source:
<Link to requirements document as provided by the requestor>

<A more detailed description of the project deliverables. The description should be written so that what the project will actually deliver is easily understood.>

< If there is ambiguity, then also explicitly state what the project will **not** deliver.>

Assumptions and restrictions

Assumptions:

<State any assumptions upon which the project is based>

Restrictions:

<State any restrictions to the project>

Critical success factors

- <List any factors which will directly affect the critical path of the project>

Critical risk factors

- <List any project specific critical risk factors which the project sponsor would need to be aware of>

Opportunities

- <List any project opportunities which the project sponsor should be aware of>

Project Schedule

Project start:	YYYY-MM-DD	
Milestone		**Due Date**
<Milestone 1>		YYYY-MM-DD
<Milestone 2>		
<...>		
Project end:	YYYY-MM-DD	

STEERING BOARD REPORT TEMPLATE

The steering board report is the most important report that a project manager will provide on a regular basis. The template shown below includes all the most important information that needs to be presented to the project sponsor. There are also additional templates at the end of this section that can be included in the report. These are meant for requesting additional support, a decision from the project sponsor, or a scope change.

The steering board report template presented here is in a slide format. Often the report is presented using a projector or a computer screen, so that a slide format is appropriate. The template below could easily be adjusted to a paper format, if this would be preferred by the project sponsor or the organization.

<Project Name>
PM: <Project Manager>

Project Scope
Summary

Project Description	Project Milestones / Activities	Due Date
<Short project description>	<Milestone 1>	YYYY-MM-TT
	<Milestone 2>	
	<Milestone 3>	
Project Goals		
<Goal 1>		
<Goal 2>		
<Goal 3>		

<Project Name>
PM: <Project Manager>

Project Status: ⊙○○
Support from SB requested: No
Scope Change request: No

Current Milestones / Activities	Date	Status ●○○	Date	Achieved Results
Bla bla black sheep	YY-MM-TT		YY-MM-DD	Bla bla black sheep : Part 3

Risks & Issues	Measures taken	Due Date
Bla bla white sheep	Dye wool black	YY-MM-DD

Usage Notes for the Steering Board Template:

The Project Scope slide:

The purpose of this part of the report is to ensure that the project scope is always available during the steering board meeting. This helps to prevent scope slip. Only a summary of the scope is required here, with the major milestones. If there are concerns about the exact scope of the project, the scope statement can always be reviewed.

Include all the major project milestones. When a milestone is completed, highlight it in some simple way. (For example, set the background to a different color, change the text color, cross out the text.)

Complete the scope slide of the report once at the start of the project. Only make a change to this part of the report if a change is approved by both the project sponsor and the project manager.

The Status Summary Slide:

The purpose of this part of the report is to provide a quick but accurate overview of the project status to the project sponsor.

Only list the current milestones and activities. Include the relevant dates from the scope statement or current project schedule.

Using traffic lights (red, green, yellow) provides an easily understood overview of the project status. It is important to use clear definitions for the traffic lights, such as:

- Green: Activity according to plan
- Yellow: The project has some issues, but the issues can be resolved using the resources available to the project
- Red: The project has some issues which it cannot solve with the available resources, and support is required from the project sponsor or steering board

When filling in the achieved results, list the most recently completed three or four work packages.

Under risks and issues, list the top risks or issues which are affecting the project now and the countermeasures taken to mitigate / resolve them. If no issues or risks are affecting the project, leave this section blank.

Below are the templates for requesting additional support, a decision from the project sponsor, and a change request. Include these in the report if they are needed.

<Project>   Support Request

Issue

<Description of issue>

<Summary of steps already taken to resolve the issue>

Support Requested

<What support should the steering board provide?>
<What is the likely impact of not providing the requested support?>
<What are the implications (cost, time, etc.) of providing the requested support>

<Project>   Decision Request

Decision Summary

<Summary of the decision requested>

Available Options

<Brief Summary of the available options>

<What is the impact of the available options with regard to the project and/or the organisation as a whole?>

<Optional: Recommendation>

<Project>   Scope Change Request

Background	Project Impact
Requestor: Summary of Change request: Why can this not be implemented in next release?	Project delivery delay: Additional costs: Additional required resources:

Index

5W plus H 268

Analogous Estimation 283

Approval

    Commit to Plan 76

    Process 64

Authority 333

Burndown Chart 364

Business Case

    Detailed 94, 168

    Outline 74, 131

Closure

    Incomplete or Failed Projects 250

    Practice 241

    Theory 113

Commitment

    Execution 173

Communication

    Definition 342

    Practice 234

    Tools 342

Communication Plan 90

    Practice 163

Template...374

Consolidated Project Report 38

Contingency Cost...319

    Calculation...324

Cost Management..105

    Tools..350

Cost Tracking..138

Crashing...190

Creative Process...254

Creativity...254

    5W plus H...268

    Framework...256

    Mind Mapping 264

    Reversal 267

Critical Path..104

    Network Diagram 303

Decision

    Requesting...227

De-escalation Management..222

Deliverables 80

    Defining...143

Delivery Schedule...88, 156

Delphi Method 284

Earned Value Management..352

Estimation...149

    Analogous...283

    Delphi Method...284

    Expert 290

    Parametric 286

Techniques 280

Three Point.. 292

EVM

Earned Value Management.. 352

Execution

Completion.. 112

Theory 102

Execution and Monitoring

Practice 177

Process... 102, 177

Theory 99

Expert Estimation 290

Fast Tracking... 189

Formal Handover 114

Gantt Chart.. 305

Usage... 158

Goals...67, 123

Evaluation... 142

Hard Skills 340

Improvements 206

Initiation

Practice 120

Theory 66

Internal and External View... 80

Issue

Definition 309

Most Frequent... 216

Kick-Off Meeting 101, 180

Kipling Method... 268

Knowledge Management...49

Late Projects 188

Lessons Learned 115, 243

    Meeting.. 245

Management

    Definition...5

Matrix organisation 22

    Resource conflicts 29, 46

Meetings

    Frequency of.. 124

Mind Mapping.. 264

Monitoring

    Practice.. 186

    Theory 103

Motivation.. 235

Network Diagram 300

Operations

    Definition...4

Opportunity

    Definition.. 309

Parametric Estimation 286

People Management.. 332

Planning

    Accuracy 140

    Output..78

    Overall Goal..78

    Theory 78

Power.. 333

Project

Definition 2

Project Commitment

Execution 98

Project management methodology 33

Project Management Office 20, 31

Project Management Process 63

Project Management Triangle 270

Project Manager 18

Selecting 126

Project organisation 25

Project Plan 87, 155

Project Risk Diagram 318

Project Schedule

Development 160

Tools 294

Project Sponsor 16, 52

Roles and Responsibilities 53

Project Team 19

Projects

Late 188

Quality 128

Reporting 208

Resource

Usage over Time 89

Resource Availability

Practice 151

Theory 86

Resource Estimation

Practice 149

Theory 85

Resource Plan...88

Practice...162

Reversal 267

Risk

Assesment Intial...165

Contingency Cost 319

Definition..309

Identification 313

Project Risk Diagram 318

Quantification...316

Risk Management 42, 92, 106, 309

Risk Mitigation...328

Scope Change..203, 205

Scope Slip 174

Scope Statement...96, 170

Creating...171

Skill Management 339

SMCR

Communication Model 344

Soft Skills 341

Stakeholders 72, 133

List..133

Standards 44

Steering Board Report

Template..377

Task Dependencies 296

Team Building...231, 335

Team Management 231

Three Point Estimation.. 292

Time Estimation.. 244

Time Management.. 366

WBS

    Usage...84, 148

    Work Breakdown Structure 273

Work Breakdown Structure 273

Work Package

    Distribution... 183

    Template 372

www.ingramcontent.com/pod-product-compliance
Lightning Source LLC
Chambersburg PA
CBHW060316200326
41519CB00011BA/1744

* 9 7 8 3 9 4 6 1 6 0 5 0 2 *